PENPALS
for
Handwriting

Years 5 & 6 Teacher's Book
(9–11 years)

Gill Budgell   Kate Ruttle

Series Consultants
Sue Palmer   Professor Rhona Stainthorp

Contents

CAMBRIDGE   HITACHI
www.cambridge-hitachi.com

Scope and sequence

Foundation 1/3–5 years

DEVELOPING GROSS MOTOR SKILLS
1 The vocabulary of movement
2 Large movements
3 Responding to music

DEVELOPING FINE MOTOR SKILLS
4 Hand and finger play
5 Making and modelling
6 Links to art
7 Using one-handed tools and equipment

DEVELOPING PATTERNS AND BASIC LETTER MOVEMENTS
8 Pattern-making
9 Responding to music
10 Investigating straight line patterns
11 Investigating loops
12 Investigating circles
13 Investigating angled patterns
14 Investigating eights and spirals

Foundation 2/Primary 1

Term 2
1 Introducing long ladder letters: *l, i, t, u, j, y*
2 Practising long ladder letters: *l, i*
3 Practising long ladder letters: *t, u*
4 Practising long ladder letters: *j, y*
5 Practising all the long ladder letters
6 Introducing one-armed robot letters: *r, b, n, h, m, k, p*
7 Practising one-armed robot letters: *b, n*
8 Practising one-armed robot letters: *h, m*
9 Practising one-armed robot letters: *k, p*
10 Practising all the one-armed robot letters
11 Introducing capitals for one-armed robot letters: *R, B, N, H, M, K, P*
12 Introducing capitals for long ladder letters: *L, I, T, U, J, Y*

Term 3
13 Introducing curly caterpillar letters: *c, a, d, o, s, g, q, e, f*
14 Practising curly caterpillar letters: *a, d*
15 Practising curly caterpillar letters: *o, s*
16 Practising curly caterpillar letters: *g, q*
17 Practising curly caterpillar letters: *e, f*
18 Practising all the curly caterpillar letters
19 Introducing zig-zag monster letters: *z, v, w, x*
20 Practising zig-zag monster letters: *v, w, x*
21 Introducing capitals for curly caterpillar letters: *C, A, D, O, S, G, Q, E, F*
22 Introducing capitals for zig-zag monster letters: *Z, V, W, X*
23 Exploring *ch, th* and *sh*

Year 1/Primary 2

Term 1
1 Letter formation practice: long ladder family
2 Letter formation practice: one-armed robot family
3 Letter formation practice: curly caterpillar family
4 Letter formation practice: zig-zag monster family
5 Practising the vowels: *i*
6 Practising the vowels: *u*
7 Practising the vowels: *a*
8 Practising the vowels: *o*
9 Practising the vowels: *e*
10 Letter formation practice: capital letters

Term 2
11 Introducing diagonal join to ascender: joining *at, all*
12 Practising diagonal join to ascender: joining *th*
13 Practising diagonal join to ascender: joining *ch*
14 Practising diagonal join to ascender: joining *cl*
15 Introducing diagonal join, no ascender: joining *in, im*
16 Practising diagonal join, no ascender: joining *cr, tr, dr*
17 Practising diagonal join, no ascender: joining *lp, mp*
18 Introducing diagonal join, no ascender, to an anticlockwise letter: joining *id, ig*
19 Practising diagonal join, no ascender, to an anticlockwise letter: joining *nd, ld*
20 Practising diagonal join, no ascender, to an anticlockwise letter: joining *ng*

Term 3
21 Practising diagonal join, no ascender: joining *ee*
22 Practising diagonal join, no ascender: joining *ai, ay*
23 Practising diagonal join, no ascender: joining *ime, ine*
24 Introducing horizontal join, no ascender: joining *op, oy*
25 Practising horizontal join, no ascender: joining *one, ome*
26 Introducing horizontal join, no ascender, to an anticlockwise letter: joining *oa, og*
27 Practising horizontal join, no ascender, to an anticlockwise letter: joining *wa, wo*
28 Introducing horizontal join to ascender: joining *ol, ot*
29 Practising horizontal join to ascender: joining *wh, oh*
30 Introducing horizontal and diagonal joins to ascender, to an anticlockwise letter: joining *of, if*
31 Assessment

Year 2/Primary 3

Term 1
1 How to join in a word: high-frequency words
2 Introducing the break letters: *j, g, x, y, z, b, f, p, q, r, s*
3 Practising diagonal join to ascender in words: *eel, eet*
4 Practising diagonal join, no ascender, in words: *a_e*
5 Practising diagonal join, no ascender, to an anticlockwise letter in words: *ice, ide*
6 Practising horizontal join, no ascender, in words: *ow, ou*
7 Practising horizontal join, no ascender, in words: *oy, oi*
8 Practising horizontal join, no ascender, to an anticlockwise letter in words: *oa, ode*
9 Practising horizontal join to ascender in words: *ole, obe*
10 Practising horizontal join to ascender in words: *ook, ool*

Term 2
11 Practising diagonal join to r: *ir, ur, er*
12 Practising horizontal join to r: *or, oor*
13 Introducing horizontal join from r to ascender: *url, irl, irt*
14 Introducing horizontal join from r: *ere*
15 Practising joining to and from r: *air*
16 Introducing diagonal join to s: *dis*
17 Introducing horizontal join to s: *ws*
18 Introducing diagonal join from s to ascender: *sh*
19 Introducing diagonal join from s, no ascender: *si, su, se, sp, sm*
20 Introducing horizontal join from r to an anticlockwise letter: *rs*

Term 3
21 Practising diagonal join to an anticlockwise letter: *ea, ear*
22 Introducing horizontal join to and from f to ascender: *ft, fl*
23 Introducing horizontal join from f, no ascender: *fu, fr*
24 Introducing *qu* (diagonal join, no ascender)
25 Introducing *rr* (horizontal join, no ascender)
26 Introducing *ss* (diagonal join, no ascender, to an anticlockwise letter)
27 Introducing *ff* (horizontal join to ascender)
28 Capital letter practice: height of ascenders and capitals
29 Assessment
30 Assessment

Scope and sequence

Year 3 / Primary 4

Term 1
1 Revising joins in a word: long vowel phonemes
2 Revising joins in a word: *le*
3 Revising joins in a word: *ing*
4 Revising joins in a word: high-frequency words
5 Revising joins in a word: new vocabulary
6 Revising joins in a word: *un, de*
7 Revising joins to and from s: *dis*
8 Revising joins to and from r: *re, pre*
9 Revising joins to and from f: *ff*
10 Revising joins: *qu*

Term 2
11 Introducing joining b and p: diagonal join, no ascender, *bi, bu, pi, pu*
12 Practising joining b and p: diagonal join, no ascender, to an anticlockwise letter, *ba, bo, pa, po*
13 Practising joining b and p: diagonal join to ascender, *bl, ph*
14 Relative sizes of letters: silent letters
15 Parallel ascenders: high-frequency words
16 Parallel descenders: adding *y* to words
17 Relative size and consistency: *ly, less, ful*
18 Relative size and consistency: capitals
19 Speed and fluency practice: *er, est*
20 Speed and fluency practice: opposites

Term 3
21 Consistency in spacing: *mis, anti, ex*
22 Consistency in spacing: *non, co*
23 Consistency in spacing: apostrophes
24 Layout, speed and fluency practice: address
25 Layout, speed and fluency practice: dialogue
26 Layout, speed and fluency practice: poem
27 Layout, speed and fluency practice: letter
28 Handwriting style
29 Assessment
30 Handwriting style

Year 4 / Primary 5

Term 1
1 Revising joins in a word: *ness, ship*
2 Revising joins in a word: *ing, ed*
3 Revising joins in a word: *s*
4 Revising joins in a word: *ify*
5 Revising joins in a word: *nn, mm, ss*
6 Revising parallel ascenders: *tt, ll, bb*
7 Revising parallel ascenders and descenders: *pp, ff*
8 Revising joins to an anticlockwise letter: *cc, dd*
9 Revising break letters: alphabetical order
10 Linking spelling and handwriting: related words

Term 2
11 Introducing sloped writing
12 Parallel ascenders: *al, ad, af*
13 Parallel descenders and break letters: *ight, ough*
14 Size, proportion and spacing: *ious*
15 Size, proportion and spacing: *able, ful*
16 Size, proportion and spacing: *fs, ves*
17 Speed and fluency: abbreviations for notes
18 Speed and fluency: notemaking
19 Speed and fluency: drafting
20 Speed and fluency: lists

Term 3
21 Size, proportion and spacing: *v, k*
22 Size, proportion and spacing: *ic, ist*
23 Size, proportion and spacing: *ion*
24 Size, proportion and spacing: contractions
25 Speed and fluency: *ible, able*
26 Speed and fluency: diminutives
27 Print alphabet
28 Print capitals
29 Assessment
30 Presentational skills: font styles

Years 5 & 6 / Primary 6 & 7

Year 5 Handwriting
1 Revision: practising sloped writing
2 Revision: practising the joins
3 Developing style for speed: joining from *t*
4 Developing style for speed: looping from *g, j* and *y*
5 Developing style for speed: joining from *f*
6 Developing style for speed: joining from *s*
7 Developing style for speed: writing *v, w, x* and *z* at speed
8 Developing style for speed: pen breaks in longer words
9 Different styles for different purposes
10 Assessment

Year 5 Project work
11 Haiku project: making notes
12 Haiku project: organising ideas
13 Haiku project: producing a draft
14 Haiku project: publishing the haiku
15 Haiku project: evaluation
16 Letter project: making notes
17 Letter project: structuring an argument
18 Letter project: producing a draft
19 Letter project: publishing a letter
20 Letter project: evaluation

Year 6 Handwriting
21 Self-assessment: evaluating handwriting
22 Self-assessment: checking the joins
23 Self-assessment: consistency of size
24 Self-assessment: letters resting on baseline
25 Self-assessment: ascenders and descenders
26 Self-assessment: consistency of size of capitals and ascenders
27 Writing at speed: inappropriate closing of letters
28 Writing at speed: identifying unclosed letters
29 Writing at speed: spacing within words
30 Writing at speed: spacing between words

Year 6 Project work
31 Playscript project: collecting information
32 Playscript project: recording ideas
33 Playscript project: producing a draft
34 Playscript project: publishing a playscript
35 Playscript project: evaluation
36 Information notice project: collecting and organising information
37 Information notice project: organising information
38 Information notice project: producing a draft
39 Information notice project: publishing a notice
40 Information notice project: evaluation

Even in this computer-literate age, good handwriting remains fundamental to our children's educational achievement. *Penpals for Handwriting* will help you teach children to develop fast, fluent, legible handwriting. The rationale for introducing joining is fully explained on page 11. This carefully structured handwriting scheme can also make a difference to overall attainment in writing.

Traditional principles in the contemporary classroom

We believe that:

1 A flexible, fluent and legible handwriting style empowers children to write with confidence and creativity. This is an entitlement that needs skilful teaching.

2 Handwriting is a developmental process with its own distinctive stages of sequential growth. We have identified five stages that form the basic organisational structure of *Penpals*:

1 Readiness for handwriting; gross and fine motor skills leading to pattern-making and letter formation (Foundation / 3–5 years)
2 Beginning to join (Key Stage 1 / 5–7 years)
3 Securing the joins (Key Stage 1 and lower Key Stage 2 / 5–9 years)
4 Practising speed and fluency (lower Key Stage 2 / 7–9 years)
5 Presentation skills (upper Key Stage 2 / 9–11 years)

3 Handwriting must be actively taught; this can be done in association with spelling. Learning to associate the kinaesthetic handwriting movement with the visual letter pattern and the aural phonemes will help children with learning to spell.

A practical approach

Penpals offers a practical approach to support the delivery of handwriting teaching in the context of the modern curriculum:

● **Time** *Penpals'* focus on whole-class teaching, with key teaching points clearly identified, allows effective teaching in the time available.
● **Planning** *Penpals* helps with long-, medium- and short-term planning for each key stage, correlated to national guidelines.
● **Practice** *Penpals* offers Photocopy Masters (PCMs) for pupil practice of specific handwriting issues and practice of handwriting in project work.
● **Revision** *Penpals* offers opportunities for record-keeping, review and assessment throughout the course and is in line with SATs requirements which assess handwriting in the context of general writing.
● **Motivation** The *Penpals* materials are attractive and well designed. They were written with the support of handwriting experts to stimulate and motivate children.
● **ICT** Use the *Penpals* CD-ROMs to enrich and extend children's handwriting experiences.

A few words from the experts...

Sue Palmer *Literacy specialist and educational writer*

Penpals materials provide everything necessary for structured teaching of handwriting in the junior years. Frequent links to other literacy objectives for the age group mean handwriting lessons also become an opportunity to revise other aspects of writing at word, sentence and text level.

Professor Rhona Stainthorp *Professor, Institute of Education, University of Reading*

We now know that if children are to achieve comfortable, legible, flexible handwriting styles, they need to be taught to form and join each letter efficiently. *Penpals* sets out to achieve this. Children need good models to copy, lots of practice and feedback to help them fine-tune their performance.

If the practice element of letter formation includes the practice of spelling patterns, as in *Penpals*, the resultant pedagogy addresses two of the essential sub-skills of good written communication, namely handwriting and spelling.

Efficient handwriting leads to higher quality writing.

Dr Rosemary Sassoon

The Sassoon family of typefaces has been used throughout this scheme. Many people might therefore describe them as the model but they are typefaces, not exactly a handwriting model. No hand could copy them exactly and be so consistent and invariable. Equally, no typeface, however many alternative letters and joins are built in to a font, can be quite as flexible as handwritten letters. Our letters represent the movement, proportions and clear characteristics of basic separate and joined letters. It is likely that every teacher will produce his or her own slightly different version on the whiteboard, and pupils will then do likewise. It matters little if the slant or proportions of a child's writing differ slightly from any model. We are not teaching children to be forgers. We are equipping them with an efficient, legible handwriting that will serve them all their life – one that suits their hand and their personality. Flexibility is stressed throughout this scheme.

Links to national guidelines

Penpals for Handwriting: Years 5 & 6 supports many National Guidelines including:

- the *National Curriculum for England and Wales*;
- *Primary Framework for literacy and mathematics* (Primary National Strategy 2006): handwriting is specifically mentioned in the 'Presentation' strand of the *Framework*;
- *English Language 5–14 Guidelines* (The Scottish Office Education Department);
- *The Northern Ireland Curriculum: Primary* (CCEA).

Aims of *Penpals*

Through the supportive context of whole-class teaching leading to independent writing, *Penpals* develops:

- vocabulary for talking about letter formation and joining;
- strong links between spelling patterns and handwriting practice;
- efficient pencil hold and good posture;
- an emphasis on refining handwriting joins and on developing legibility, speed and fluency;
- consideration of different styles of writing for different purposes;
- awareness of presentational issues.

Penpals in Years 5 & 6 (Primary 6 & 7)

These handwriting resources are designed to:

- provide a visually stimulating way of demonstrating all the basic principles of developing effective handwriting;
- provide samples of children's handwriting for analysis and discussion;
- give children the skills and practice necessary to write with increased speed and fluency;
- teach children how to use different styles of handwriting for different purposes, including presentation.

By Y5/P6, most children are writing fluently and are joining their writing, when appropriate, for most of their cross-curricular work. The handwriting units for Y5&6 / P6&7 do not teach new joins; the emphasis is on increased speed and on developing presentation skills. At the end of the primary school, overall assessment of writing (including SATs) covers assessment of handwriting, so it is crucial that children are able to write quickly and legibly.

In KS2 SATs, 3 marks out of a total of 28 marks from the longer written task, and 50 marks from writing, are assigned to handwriting.

Classroom organisation

The ideal classroom organisation for teaching *Penpals* is to have the children sitting at desks or tables so that they can all see the interactive whiteboard or overhead screen. Each child needs a dry-wipe board (preferably with guidelines) and a marker pen, or pencil and paper.

Timing the sessions

The *Penpals* Years 5 & 6 CD-ROM and Years 5 & 6 OHTs together provide a thorough and flexible bank of whole-class resources to support your teaching of handwriting. Choose the resources that best suit your literacy planning and the needs of your class.

- The CD-ROM focuses on reinforcing correct letter and join formation, and developing presentation skills, through demonstration and evaluation of handwriting samples.
- The OHTs focus on developing style and fluency, self-assessment and handwriting projects.

Each CD-ROM activity, and each *Developing speed and fluency* or *Assessing and improving handwriting* OHT unit, should last for about 15 minutes.

The *Project* units (11–20 and 31–40) are suitable for teaching over a longer period of time. Once you have determined which area of the curriculum is to provide the subject matter for the project, you could introduce the units, as appropriate, at the beginning of relevant sessions.

The PCMs in this book provide independent work, including evaluations, that should take about 15 minutes.

Penpals for Handwriting: Y5&6 © Gill Budgell (Frattempo) and Kate Ruttle 2009

Use the CD-ROM units to consolidate and develop the basic principles of effective and efficient handwriting and to augment your teaching using the OHTs.

Basics

1. Letter formation: *l* family
2. Letter formation: *r* family
3. Letter formation: *c* family
4. Letter formation: *z* family
5. Letter formation: *L* family
6. Letter formation: *R* family
7. Letter formation: *C* family
8. Letter formation: *Z* family
9. Letter formation at speed
10. Number formation
11. Joining: diagonal joins
12. Joining: horizontal joins
13. Joining: tricky joins
14. Joining at speed
15. Style at speed: variations on *f, g, s, t, y*
16. Style at speed: variations on *j, v, w, x, z*
17. Letter size: consistency of lower case letters
18. Letter size: comparison of lower case letters
19. Letter size: lower case letters and capital letters
20. Letter orientation: writing letters on the baseline
21. Letter orientation: ascenders and descenders
22. Spacing: between letters
23. Spacing: between words
24. Parallels: upright ascenders and descenders
25. Parallels: sloping ascenders and descenders
26. Self-assessment: handwriting check-list

Presentation

27. Writing for different purposes
28. Lettering styles: capital letters
29. Labelling: print alphabet
30. Labelling: diagrams
31. Pattern making: geometric patterns
32. Pattern making: symbols and maps

The emphasis throughout is on developing fast and fluent handwriting through addressing common weaknesses.

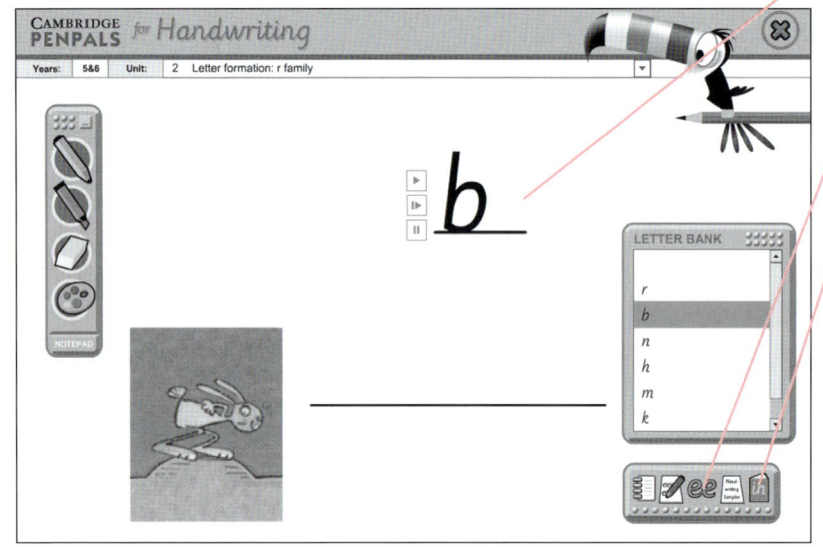

Timer appears in units related to developing speed.

Toolbar includes a pen that you can use to trace over word bank entries, or to model handwriting using the **Notepad**.

Letter animations provide opportunities to demonstrate and talk about correct letter formation. Children can practise tracing and copying the letters.

Joining letter sets shows the information from the inside back cover of this book.

Library of joins contains animations showing correct formation of key joins.

Also on the CD-ROM Handwriting workouts, and video clips of arm and hand exercises are accessible from the main menu of the CD-ROM. Use these as warm-up activities for the units.

Word bank contains a list of letters, words or phrases that focus on basic handwriting issues that may be inhibiting fast and fluent writing. Click on an entry to display it on the main screen; click on the main screen version to turn it grey for tracing. Banks in other units contain other features relating to the unit content, e.g. patterns and styles.

Handwriting samples contains a selection of children's handwriting samples for each target skill to use as a basis for analysis and discussion.

Notepad provides a bank of different paper styles on which to model/practise handwriting.

Organisation of the units

The OHTs for Y5&6/P6&7 are organised in four sections, each comprising 10 units:

1–10 *Developing speed and fluency* – these units give children extensive practice in completing short written tasks within a given time, to help them to increase speed and fluency whilst maintaining legibility. They include an acknowledgement of some joining 'short-cuts' which may aid clarity in fast and fluent writing.

11–20 *Handwriting projects* – two projects, one fiction and one non-fiction, are scaffolded from early note-making activities, through developing drafts in fast and fluent handwriting, to a neat 'presentation' of the project in careful 'best' handwriting. These projects enable children to practise using different styles of handwriting for different purposes.

These two projects are linked to QCA topics recommended for children in Y5/P6.

21–30 *Assessing and improving handwriting* – these units focus on developing children's self-evaluation skills. The first unit is a self-assessment exercise and subsequent units focus on specific aspects of handwriting that have been identified as being common problems either for legibility or for an overall impression of neat, controlled handwriting.

31–40 *Handwriting projects* – two more projects, one fiction and one non-fiction. These two projects are linked to QCA topics recommended for children in Y6/P7.

This organisation is a recommendation only and the units can be introduced in the order in which they are most appropriate for your class.

Structure of the units

Units 1–10 and 21–30

For each of these units there is:

- an OHT for whole-class work
- a PCM (photocopy master) for independent work
- a teacher's page.

Whole-class session

Use the OHT to introduce the focus point of the unit. Most sessions include **Get Up and Go** opportunities for some children to demonstrate the focus and **Show Me** activities where the whole class experiment with a short sample of handwriting on their whiteboards or with pencil and paper. The emphasis is usually on developing fast and fluent handwriting. This session should include discussion and exploration of handwriting possibilities. In units where children are encouraged to experiment with alternative joins, the introductory phrase on the OHT shows the familiar joined font. The remaining text (and the PCM text) is unjoined to allow children to make decisions about which joins to use. For all other OHTs the model given uses the familiar joined font.

Whilst the main focus of the OHT is the handwriting target, an extra opportunity for consolidation of spelling work is also offered in the form of a spelling or vocabulary link.

Independent session

Let children who need practice use the PCMs for independent work. The focus of these is purely handwriting based. Each PCM has three parts:

- The main activity, usually a timed activity, which allows children to practise the handwriting focus from the whole-class session. (The suggested time for most activities is 2 minutes, but you should alter this, as appropriate for your class. If children have completed the activity in under 2 minutes, encourage them to copy the handwriting pattern or begin to complete the evaluation.)
- An evaluation section where the children are asked to consider and comment on their handwriting.
- Handwriting patterns to increase pencil control and develop fluency of movement. The pattern is shown at the top of the page and a space is left at the bottom for the children to copy it. (There are patterns for Units 1–10 and 22–30 only.)

Plenary session

Use the children's evaluation of their work, together with any issues that arose in the whole-class session, as the basis for a plenary session. This should not be simply a 'show and tell' but could include discussion and exploration of:

- any variations to traditional joins that the children have employed;
- implications for other, similar joins;
- experimentation with new joins;
- emphasis on retaining legibility, and the problems of confusing words when similar letters or joins are written too quickly;
- new, related, handwriting patterns;
- sharing evaluations, including evaluations of patterns;
- discussing length of time taken to complete the activity.

Although links to appropriate spelling and vocabulary objectives are often included in the <u>taught</u> part of each session, the independent work is often not related to the same spelling objectives. This is because the aim of the <u>independent</u> activities is to increase the speed and fluency of handwriting and children should not be focusing on copying words with challenging spelling.

Homework

An appropriate follow-up activity is always suggested for homework. These activities could also be used if opportunities for practice arise during the week at school.

Units 11–20 and 31–40

For each of these units there is:

- an OHT for the whole-class session
- a teacher's page.

Additionally, for some units, there are PCMs to support independent work.

Although the main teaching objective of *Penpals* is to develop handwriting, children also need opportunities for <u>using</u> handwriting skills in the context of real projects and for developing appropriate handwriting styles for different tasks. This is in line with the assessment of handwriting for SATs. For this reason *Penpals* includes project-based activities that scaffold the development of a cross-curricular project:

- using notes to collect and sort out ideas
- using fast and fluent writing for drafting texts
- finally presenting a 'best' version
- evaluating each of the stages.

The projects shown are intended as samples only, to give you materials to use in order to demonstrate each of the stages. Ideally, the children will then transfer the handwriting ideas and strategies to their own projects. If, however, you choose to follow through these projects, PCMs are provided for use in the note-making activities which follow up more directly on the whole-class sessions. Samples of authentic handwriting have been used on each page. They are children's handwriting and may have slight imperfections.

Homework
An appropriate follow-up activity is always suggested for homework. These activities could also be used if opportunities for practice arise during the week at school.

Differentiation

Differentiation using *Penpals* can be achieved in a number of ways:

- Children working individually with a Teaching Assistant may benefit from additional practice on dry-wipe boards.
- Children who need extra reinforcement will benefit from working independently through the OHT activity. Simply photocopy the OHT, reducing to A5 if appropriate. You may allow the children to work on the OHT but be aware that different handwriting skills are then called into play.
- Children who are not yet joining securely will benefit from revisiting units in earlier *Penpals* books or CD-ROMs or from spending additional time working on activities generated in the revision units (Units 1 and 2).
- Some children will benefit from using the guidelines which show an appropriate slope (see page 64).
- For project work, let children work in pairs. Less confident children may scribe for the notes – when spelling is less important but reading demands are higher. All children should be expected to make the presentation document.
- Once children have completed Unit 21 (self-assessment) it will be possible to identify those who have no need to complete Units 22–30. These children can be given additional activities to practise writing at speed.
- Higher-achieving children can be challenged by higher expectations of control and evenness of letters.

Assessment and record-keeping

On-going formative assessment

The most effective assessment of handwriting is on-going assessment because this gives you the chance to spot any errors or inconsistencies that are likely to impede a fast, fluent hand in the future. Be especially aware of left-handers and the difference between a pencil hold that will seriously limit their success in the future and one that has been found to work efficiently.

At Key Stage 2, a start of year assessment PCM is provided at the beginning of each book (see page 9). This assesses the previous year's work and gives an indication of what needs to be consolidated before beginning new work.

Most of the units on the CD-ROM and in this book encourage the children to develop self- and peer-assessment skills through formative self- and peer-evaluation.

Record-keeping

- The best record of what children have achieved will be in their writing books and the *Penpals* PCMs. These will provide a useful record of achievement to share with parents and colleagues.
- The Contents page can be photocopied and used with highlighting pens and dates to keep a record of which units have been completed. You may find it helpful to use a 'traffic light' system (green highlighter pen for 'achieved', yellow for 'not totally secure' and pink for 'not achieved') to highlight units you need to revisit with individuals, groups or the whole class.

Beginning of year assessment

Name ....   Date ....

Copy this sentence.

In Year 4 I learned how to slope my writing and to think about size, spacing, speed and fluency.

_____

_____

Make a list of things you need for swimming.

_____   _____

_____   _____

_____   _____

Now abbreviate the words in your list.

_____

In capital letters write out the signs you would expect to see at a swimming pool.

_____   _____

_____   _____

Now write out these signs in print.

_____   _____

_____   _____

9

Glossary of key terms

Talking about handwriting

Throughout *Penpals* it has been assumed that correct terminology should be used as soon as possible.

Terms used in *Penpals* include:

- **Gross motor skills, fine motor skills.**
- **Lower case** letter.
- **Capital letter** is used in preference to 'upper case letter'.
- **Short letter** is the term used to describe a letter with no ascender or descender.
- **Letter with an ascender, letter with a descender.**
- **Flick** is used to describe exit strokes (note that *t* finishes with a curl to the right rather than merely an exit flick).
- **Curves** is used to describe descenders on letters (*y, j, g, f*).
- **Cross bar** is used to describe the left-to-right line on *t* and *f*. It may also be used in relation to letters that feature a left-to-right horizontal line (e.g. *e* and *z*).
- **Diagonal join to ascender** (e.g. *at*), **diagonal join (no ascender)** (e.g. *du*), **diagonal join to an anticlockwise letter** (e.g. *ho*).
- **Horizontal join to ascender** (e.g. *oh*), **horizontal join (no ascender)** (e.g. *re*), **horizontal join to an anticlockwise letter** (e.g. *wo*).
- Other important terminology used throughout *Penpals* includes **vertical, parallel, joined, sloped.**

Activities

- **Show Me** This is the term used to describe a practice activity. Children write on a dry-wipe board.
- **Get Up and Go** This describes an activity where a child is asked to come up and point out a word or letter pattern on the OHT.

Different styles of handwriting identified in the projects

Note-making – quick writing, often including abbreviations, which needs to be legible to the writer only.

Fast and fluent – the most useful style of handwriting. It must be neat and legible to all readers.

Best writing – only used for presentations. Likely to be slow and careful. Appearance and legibility are paramount.

Notes on formation of specific letters and joins

Correct letter formation can be demonstrated using the **Show alphabet** section on any of the F1 to Y4 CD-ROMs.

- *k* – the use of the curly form of *k*, as opposed to the straight *k*, is recommended by handwriting experts because its flowing form lends itself more naturally to joining. It is also more easily distinguished from the capital letter.
- *o* – there is no exit stroke from the lower case *o* when it is not joined. Unlike the flick at the bottom of letters like *n* and *l*, the exit stroke from the *o* is not an integral part of the letter, but simply a mechanism for joining.
- *e, s* – two different forms of *e* (*e / e*) and *s* (*s / s*) are used in order to show children how they alter when other letters are joined to them.
- *f, r, q, s* – letters that the children are taught to join in Y2/P3.
- *b* and *p* – letters that the children are taught to join in Y3/P4.
- *g, j, y* – there is some exploration of looping *g, j* and *y* in Y5&6/P6&7.
- *x* and *z* – we do not join to or from *x* or *z* as these are uncomfortable joins that often result in the malformation of both the joining letter and the *x* or *z*. Also, handwriting is generally faster and more legible if it is not continuously joined. However, as children develop their handwriting style they may begin to experiment with joining to *x* and *z*. As long as it is comfortable, fluent and legible, they should be encouraged to continue.

Capitals

It is generally agreed that there is no right or wrong way to form capitals. However, there is a general principle of forming them from top to bottom and left to right wherever possible. As skills and confidence develop, left-handers may well form capitals differently (they have a tendency to go from right to left, for example). This should not be an issue as capitals are never joined.

- **Capital *Y*:** the use of a central stalk (as opposed to a slanting stalk) is recommended as once children have completed the 'v' form at the top of the letter, they have a clear starting point for the downwards stroke. This formation also distinguishes the capital letter from the lower case letter and retains its shape when written at speed.
- **Capital *G*:** this form of *G* is recommended as the correct handwriting form of the letter. Variations which include a vertical line (*G*) are font forms.
- **Capital *H*:** the formation of *H* using two down strokes followed by the horizontal stroke from left to right is recommended. The alternative (one down stroke followed by a horizontal and a further down stroke) can quickly resemble the letter *M* when written at speed.
- **Capital *K*:** the formation of *K* with two pencil strokes rather than three is recommended as it is more fluently formed when writing at speed.

In order to promote fluent handwriting and to support the early stages of spelling, some handwriting joins are introduced in Y1/P2 as soon as all individual letter formation is secure.

By the time they are using the Y5&6/P6&7 resources, children should be becoming secure and confident with the common joins and beginning to use them for all 'neat' writing activities. The emphasis in these resources is on developing an even, fluent handwriting style, ensuring consistency in size and proportion of letters, and the spacing between letters and words.

Progression in the introduction of joins

Y1/P2 In these resources only two or three letters in a word are joined. The words on the CD-ROM and in the Big Book and the Practice Book feature the focus join for the teaching unit.

Y2/P3 As more joins are introduced, children are given opportunities to practise familiar joins which are not the focus of the unit. During the year, children are expected to begin to join all the letters in a short word, or to join letter patterns which can support spelling choices.

Y3/P4 All the basic joins will now be familiar. In these resources, children are asked to practise 'tricky joins' and to begin to develop fluent, even handwriting. An emphasis on spacing between letters and words, consistency of letter size, and parallel ascenders and descenders helps children to present their work well.

Y4/P5 Children are introduced to a sloped style of writing and are expected to write mostly in pen. Children are also introduced to the print alphabet for purposes such as captions, labels, headings and posters.

Y5&6/P6&7 The CD-ROM consolidates joining and presentation skills. Two sets of OHTs are provided for each of these year groups. One set focuses on speed and fluency plus assessing and improving handwriting whilst the other develops handwriting and presentation skills across the curriculum through project work.

Defining the joins

(See the inside back cover of this Teacher's Book for a full list of letter patterns requiring each of the joins.)

The two basic join types

- **Diagonal join** (e.g. *at*) (introduced in Y1/P2, Unit 11): this is the most common join. It starts from the final flick on the baseline (or 'curl' in the case of the letter *t*). Letters that come before a diagonal join are: *a*, *b*, *c*, *d*, *e*, *h*, *i*, *k*, *l*, *m*, *n*, *p*, *s*, *t*, *u* (and *q*, in which the flick begins below the baseline).
- **Horizontal join** (e.g. *oh*) (introduced in Y1/P2, Unit 24): this join is formed from letters that finish at the top of the letter rather than at the baseline. Letters that come before a horizontal join are: *f*, *o*, *r*, *v*, *w*.

Variations on the join types

Penpals uses three subsets of the main joins: join to a letter with an ascender, join to a letter with no ascender, join to a letter that begins with an anticlockwise movement. Since the last subset involves stopping the pencil and reversing the direction of movement, these are called *diagonal join to an anticlockwise letter* and *horizontal join to an anticlockwise letter*. Joins to anticlockwise letters are trickier to teach and need more practice than straightforward horizontal and diagonal joins. These joins tend to 'decay' when children begin to write more quickly.

- **Diagonal join to a letter with an ascender** (e.g. *ub*) (introduced in Y1/P2, Unit 11): this is a variation of the diagonal join. It must be steeper, otherwise the spacing between letters would be too great.
- **Diagonal join to an anticlockwise letter** (e.g. *ho*) (introduced in Y1/P2, Unit 18): joining with a diagonal join to the anticlockwise letters in the 'curly caterpillar' family involves stopping the hand movement and reversing it. This can be a tricky join and it decays easily in fast writing.
- **Horizontal join to an anticlockwise letter** (e.g. *wo*) (introduced in Y1/P2, Unit 26): joining from a horizontal join to an anticlockwise letter involves a reversal.
- **Horizontal join to a letter with an ascender** (e.g. *oh*) (introduced in Y1/P2, Unit 28): this is a version of a horizontal join.
- **Break letters** (introduced in Y2/P3): these are letters from which no join has yet been taught. (See notes on page 10.)
- **Diagonal join with initial reversal** *s* (introduced in Y2/P3, Unit 16) and the letters *b* and *p* (introduced in Y3/P4, Unit 11): these are tricky to join from but many handwriting experts, including Rosemary Sassoon, believe that children should be taught to join from them. As the letter is completed, the pencil is moving to the left, so to begin the join, the hand movement must be stopped and reversed.

Correct formation of key joins can be demonstrated using the **Library of joins** section on the CD-ROM.

When you introduce *Penpals* into your school, it is important to ensure that all the staff in the school follow the scheme. Suggestions are given on page 11 to support the introduction of the programme throughout the school as there may be some issues for children who have not met joining before. To do this, it may be useful to hold an INSET staff meeting. The following pages in this book are photocopiable to make OHTs for this purpose:

- page 13 – information sheet for parents;
- page 14 – variations of the font (see above);
- page 15 – handwriting styles introduced through Y5&6/P6&7 projects;
- page 64 – photocopiable ruled sheet for handwriting practice;
- inside back cover – joining letter sets.

Suggested topics for inclusion in INSET meeting

- **Writing on lined paper** Children should be encouraged to write on lined paper from the time they begin to focus on correct letter formation and orientation. As the children's handwriting becomes more controlled, the width between the lines should decrease. It may well be that at any given time different children in your class will benefit from writing on paper with different line widths. The size of the font used throughout the programme is intended to reflect a development in handwriting. However, you should still tailor the handwriting materials to meet the needs of individual children in your class. A photocopiable sheet with lines of a suitable width is provided on page 64. Some children may prefer to write on lined paper which also includes guidelines for the height of ascenders and descenders.

- **Pencil hold** Use the pencil hold videos in the **Posture clips** section on the CD-ROM to illustrate good pencil hold. The traditionally recommended pencil hold allows children to sustain handwriting for long periods without tiring their hands. However, there are many alternative pencil holds (particularly for left-handers) and the most important thing is comfort and a grip that will be efficient under speed. Some children may benefit from triangular pencils or ordinary pencils with plastic pencil grips.

- **Posture** Use the photographs in the **Posture clips** section on the CD-ROM to illustrate good posture. A good posture and pencil hold are vital for good handwriting. Although many young children enjoy sitting on one foot, kneeling or wrapping their feet around the legs of the chair, they will find it easier to sustain good handwriting comfortably if they adopt a good posture.

- **Left-handed children** Left-handed children should not sit to the right of right-handed children as their papers will meet in the middle! Left-handed children should be taught to position their paper to the left of centre and then angle the paper for comfort as suggested below. Use the left-handed pencil hold video and posture photograph on the CD-ROM to illustrate this. There is no reason why left-handed children's handwriting should be any worse than that of right-handed children.

- **Sloped surfaces** Children who experience some motor control difficulties often benefit from writing on a slight slope. The easiest and cheapest way to provide this in the classroom is to use substantial A4 or foolscap ring-binders of which there are usually plenty in school. Commercial wooden or plastic writing slopes are also widely available.

- **Angle of paper** If children still need assistance with this then use the handwriting mats from any of the previous years of *Penpals*. These show the children how to line up the corners of their books to create a comfortable angle for writing, or how to use Blu-tack to secure paper to the mats to produce guidelines when writing on blank paper.

Penpals for Handwriting: Years 5 & 6 (9–11 years) information sheet for parents

Letter formation of capitals and lower case letters should now be familiar and secure.

Children have been introduced to the two basic join types:

- Joins from the baseline, known as **diagonal joins**, including:
  - diagonal join to a short letter, e.g. *mm, nn*
  - diagonal join to an ascender, e.g. *th, ll*
  - diagonal join to an anticlockwise letter, e.g. *ic, ss*
- Joins from the crossbar, known as **horizontal joins**, including:
  - horizontal join to a short letter, e.g. *ou, on*
  - horizontal join to an ascender, e.g. *ot, wh, fl*
  - horizontal join to an anticlockwise letter, e.g. *oo, wa, fa*

By this stage, children should be secure at joining and able to use joined up writing for most of their work. Children will be experimenting with sloping their writing and using different joins for a more mature and comfortable style and will be writing mostly in ink.

At the end of the primary phase, handwriting will be assessed in the context of general writing. It is therefore important that in Years 5 and 6 children become confident with writing appropriately in different situations.

The *Penpals* handwriting materials let children develop speed and fluency in writing. They also allow them to assess and improve their own handwriting.

There are also opportunities to practise handwriting for different purposes in projects. These include:

- note-making – quick writing
- fast and fluent writing – neat and legible to all readers
- best writing – writing for presentations.

The projects allow for the use of print letters (e.g. for labelling) and capital letters (e.g. for posters). There are both fiction and non-fiction projects.

Variations in font throughout *Penpals*

FIVE DEVELOPMENTAL PHASES	SASSOON® CAMBRIDGE JOINER	*Penpals* Progression	*Penpals* typesizes*
1 GROSS AND FINE MOTOR SKILLS AND LETTER FORMATION	 *a* *b* *c* *d*	Each letter family is introduced with finger tracing letters incorporating the letter family artwork and a starting dot. Hollow letters with starting dots and arrows to show correct letter formation are also used for finger tracing. Solid letters with starting dots support letter formation. Independent writing with exit flicks is encouraged in preparation for joining.	*a a* **Foundation 2/Primary 1** 21mm/11.5mm *a a* **Year 1/Primary 2** 17mm/8mm *a* **Year 2/Primary 3** 5.5mm
2 BEGINNING TO JOIN	*p**en*	Red is used for the focus join and joining letters to teach fluent formation.	*a* **Year 3/Primary 4** 4mm
3 SECURING THE JOINS	*secure*	Once all joins have been taught, all words are shown as joined for practice and consolidation.	*a* **Year 4 onwards/ Primary 5 onwards** sloped, 4mm
4 PRACTISING SPEED AND FLUENCY	*faster*	Children are encouraged to develop an individual style for speed and legibility.	
5 PRESENTATION SKILLS	*individual* print jokey	Further development of an individual style as well as presentation skills and techniques.	* Letters in red are for finger tracing. Letters in black are writing models.

 14

Different styles of handwriting identified in the projects for Y5&6 (9–11 years)

- **Note-making** – quick writing, often including abbreviations, which needs to be legible to the writer only.

- **Fast and fluent writing** – the most useful style of handwriting. It must be neat and legible to all readers.

- **Best writing** – only used for presentations. Likely to be slow and careful. Appearance and legibility are paramount.

- **Printing for presentation** – used for labelling, captions, posters, etc.

1 Revision: practising sloped writing

Unit focus: practising sloped writing.
Vocabulary link: synonyms.

Whole-class session — using OHT 1

- Remind the children that in Y4/P5 they learnt to write with a slope.
- Discuss the three different levels of sloping in the writing on the OHT. The first example is upright, the second is sloped to an acceptable angle, and the third is really sloped too far.
- Discuss how the guidelines help you to keep the slope even, with all the ascenders and descenders parallel.

  Show Me Ask the children to practise writing synonyms for *upset*. (Some possibilities are *sad*, *irritated*, *frustrated*, *angry*.) When they share their writing, discuss the level of slope they have used.

  Get Up and Go Ask for volunteers to come and practise writing the words on the OHT, using the guidelines for the varying degrees of slope. Discuss which they find most comfortable and easiest to do. Most will find the extremely sloped writing at the bottom uncomfortable and difficult to do, so should avoid it.

OHT 1

Independent work — using PCM for Unit 1

- Children copy out the rhyme using the sloped guidelines.
- Ask children to think about and comment on their handwriting to complete the evaluation.
- Children copy the pattern in the space at the bottom of the page.

Extra practice/Homework

- Children write words from their spelling logs that have ascenders and descenders, using the photocopiable sloped guidelines (page 64).

2 Revision: practising the joins

Unit focus: practising the joins.
Spelling link: common letter strings.

Whole-class session — using OHT 2

- Before you begin, you may wish to photocopy the joining letter sets (see the back cover) either at A5 size so that each child can have their own copy, or at A3 size to display at the front of the class.
- The letters at the top of the OHT are those that join with diagonal joins. The letters on the bottom left are those that join with horizontal joins. The letters on the bottom right are break letters. They are provided here as a ready reference.

  Show Me Ask children to practise writing some words including the common letter strings: *tion*, *sion*, *ight*, *ough*, *our*.

- Model completing some of the words in the left-hand column, and writing the complete words in the right-hand column (e.g. *station*, *occasion*, *bright*, *through*, *flour*).
- Check that children have made all the joins correctly.

  Get Up and Go Ask for volunteers to come and practise writing these words on the OHT.

OHT 2

Independent work — using PCM for Unit 2

- Children copy out the rhyme, ensuring they make all the joins correctly.
- Children complete the evaluation, identifying any joins they need to practise.
- Children copy the pattern in the space at the bottom of the page.

Extra practice/Homework

- Children choose a short piece of text (e.g. junk mail, a piece from a newspaper or TV guide, text from cereal packets) and copy it out, paying attention to slope and joins.

3 Developing style for speed: joining from t

NB: From this stage on, it is likely that children's own individual handwriting styles will be starting to develop. Models are given unjoined in order to allow children to make their own decisions.

Unit focus: alternative joins from *t* to aid speed.
Spelling link: prefixes **circum**, **trans**.

Whole-class session | using OHT 3

- Read the prefixes and the word endings. Agree which prefix goes with which word ending. (**NB:** *ference* can can be prefixed by both *circum* and *trans*.)
  Show Me Children write each word out quickly.

- Children should compare their writing with their partner. Has anything happened to their letter formation and joins under speed?

- Ask them to focus on joins from *t*. Are there any variations of the join from the curve? (For example, some children may have joined from the crossbar: *ta*.)

  Get Up and Go Ask children to write the words on the OHT. If you think it appropriate, show how you could join from the crossbar of the *t* for speed or how double *t* is sometimes joined using a single crossbar.

- Correct any variations that are not legible. Discuss the benefits of this join for speed, especially to letters with ascenders. (**NB:** Crossbar joins to *e* tend to be awkward.)

OHT 3 illustration

> 3 Developing style for speed: joining from t
>
> *circum*
> *or*
> *trans?*
>
> | port | stances |
> | late | parent |
> | ference | fer |
> | mit | navigate |

OHT **3**

Independent work | using PCM for Unit 3

- The children should copy the tongue-twister as quickly as possible (say, in two minutes or less), choosing how to join from *t*. They should then complete the evaluation.
- Children copy the pattern in the space at the bottom of the page.

Extra practice/Homework

- Children think of an alliterative phrase involving the letter *t* and at least one word with *tt*. How many times can they write it out in two minutes? They should then try writing it out neatly. Encourage them to compare the two.

---

4 Developing style for speed: looping from g, j and y

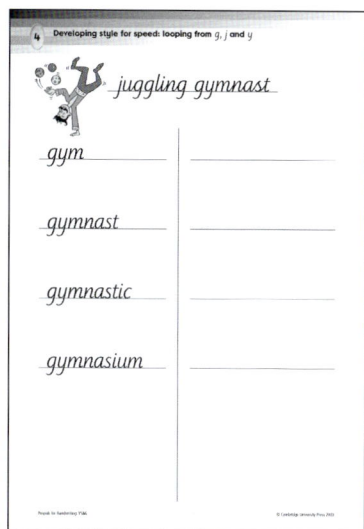

Unit focus: joins from *g*, *j*, and *y* to aid speed.
Vocabulary link: related words.

Whole-class session | using OHT 4

- Use the phrase *juggling gymnast* to introduce the unit. Read the *gym* words. Discuss the relationship between the words.
  Show Me Children write all the words as quickly as possible at least twice.

- Children should compare their writing with their partner. Has anything happened to their letter formation and joins under speed?

- Remind the children that up till now *g*, *j* and *y* have always been break letters. Ask if any children have made joins from *g* and *y*. How? (with loops: *gym*)

  Get Up and Go Ask children who have joined from *g* and *y* to demonstrate on the OHT. If no children have joined these letters, and you think it appropriate, show how you could join these letters using loops for speed.

- Correct any variations that are not legible and therefore not acceptable. Discuss the benefits of this join for speed.

OHT 4 illustration

> 4 Developing style for speed: looping from g, j and y
>
> *juggling gymnast*
>
> *gym*
>
> *gymnast*
>
> *gymnastic*
>
> *gymnasium*

OHT **4**

Independent work | using PCM for Unit 4

- Read *The Old Grey Donkey* and identify opportunities for joining from *g*, *j* and *y*.
- The children should copy the rhyme as fast as possible, joining from *g*, *j* and *y* if they want to. Ask children to complete the evaluation.
- Children copy the pattern in the space at the bottom of the page.

Extra practice/Homework

- Children think of a phrase involving the letters *g*, *j* and *y*. How many times can they write it out in two minutes? They should then try writing it out neatly and compare the two.

5 Developing style for speed: joining from *f*

Unit focus: alternative joins from *f* for speed.
Spelling link: making plurals.

Whole-class session — using OHT 5

- Use the phrase *toffee waffles* to introduce the session.
- Read the words. Agree what the plural of each one would be and ask the children to write it quickly.
  Show Me Ask the children to write the singular and plural forms of each word as quickly as possible.
- Children should compare their writing with their partner. Has anything happened to their letter formation and joins under speed?
- Remind the children that until now, *f* has always joined from the crossbar. How have they made any joins from *f*? Are there any variations from the crossbar join? Have any children joined with a loop? (some common variations, with loops and joining with a single crossbar: *ff ff*)
  Get Up and Go Ask children to demonstrate their joins on the OHT. If no children have joined using a loop, and you think it appropriate, show how you could join from *f* using a loop for speed or how double *f* is sometimes joined using a single crossbar.
- Correct any variations that are not legible. Discuss the benefits of this join for speed.

Independent work — using PCM for Unit 5

- Read the joke and identify opportunities for joining from *f*.
- The children should copy the joke as quickly as possible (say, in two minutes or less), choosing how to join from *f*.
- Ask children to complete the evaluation.
- Children copy the pattern in the space at the bottom of the page.

Extra practice/Homework

- Children think of an alliterative sentence involving the letter *f* and at least one word containing *ff*. How many times can they write it out in two minutes? They should then try writing it out neatly. Encourage them to compare the two.

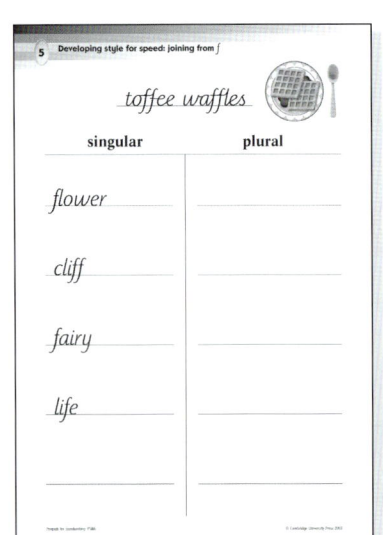

OHT **5**

6 Developing style for speed: joining from *s*

Unit focus: alternative joins from *s* for speed.
Vocabulary link: onomatopoeia.

Whole-class session — using OHT 6

- Use the phrase *splish splash!* to introduce the session.
- Read the words.
  Show Me Ask the children to write the words as quickly as possible.
- Children should compare their writing with their partner. Has anything happened to their letter formation and joins under speed?
- Remind children of the familiar join to and from *s*. How have they joined? Are there any variations from the usual letter formation and join? (for example: *ss ss ss*)
  Get Up and Go Ask children to demonstrate their joins on the OHT. If no children have joined using an alternative form of *s*, and you think it appropriate, model the alternative form.
- Correct any variations that are not legible and therefore not acceptable. Discuss the benefits of this form for speed.

Independent work — using PCM for Unit 6

- Read the tongue-twister and identify opportunities for joining from *s*.
- The children should copy the rhyme as quickly as possible (say, in two minutes or less), choosing how to join from *s*.
- Ask children to complete the evaluation.
- Children copy the pattern in the space at the bottom of the page.

Extra practice/Homework

- Children think of an alliterative sentence involving the letter *s* and at least one word containing *ss*. How many times can they write it out in two minutes? They should then try writing it out neatly. Encourage them to compare the two.

OHT **6**

7 Developing style for speed: writing v, w, x and z at speed

Unit focus: alternative forms of *v*, *w*, *x* and *z* for speed.
Spelling link: words ending in vowels other than **e**.

Whole-class session — using OHT 7

- Use the phrase *boxes of words ending in vowels* to introduce the session.
- Read the words and refer to the spelling link.
  Show Me Ask the children to write the words as quickly as possible.
- Children should compare their writing with their partner. Has anything happened to their letter formation and joins under speed?
- Remind children of the familiar forms of *v*, *w*, *x* and *z*.
- Ask them to focus in particular on the form of *v* and *w*. Are there any variations from the usual letter formation? For example, have any children written the *v* and *w* with rounded points?
- Remind them that up until now, they have not joined either to or from *x* and *z* (this can slow down their writing). Have any children tried to join them?
  Get Up and Go Ask children to demonstrate the words on the OHT. If no children have joined using the alternative forms of *x* and *z*, and you think it appropriate, model the alternative forms. (*xt z℮*)
- Correct any variations that are not legible. Discuss the benefits of these forms for speed.

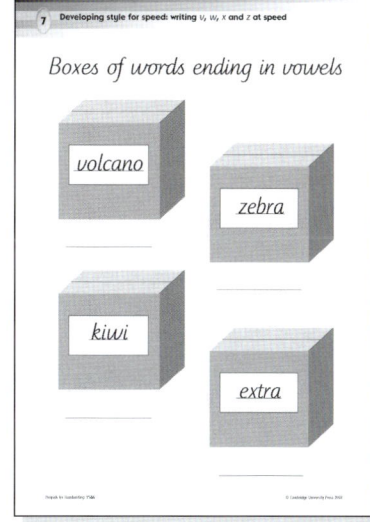

Boxes of words ending in vowels

volcano
zebra
kiwi
extra

OHT **7**

Independent work — using PCM for Unit 7

- Read the menu and identify the letters *v*, *w*, *x* and *z*. Look for stylistic use of lower case letters.
- The children should copy the menu as quickly as possible (say, in two minutes or less), choosing how to form these letters and whether to join from *x* and *z*.
- Ask children to complete the evaluation.
- Children copy the pattern in the space at the bottom of the page.

Extra practice/Homework

- Children think of a sentence involving the letters *v*, *w*, *x* and *z*. How many times can they write it in two minutes? They should try writing it out neatly, then compare the two.

8 Developing style for speed: pen breaks in longer words

Unit focus: pen breaks in longer words.
Spelling link: unstressed vowels in polysyllabic words.

NB: This unit draws on children's work on word structure, which will help them choose appropriate points to make breaks within words.

Whole-class session — using OHT 8

- Use the phrase *abominable snowman* to introduce the unit focus. Remind children that they usually don't take a pen break in the middle of the word. Discuss where you might take a pen break (e.g. before *able* and *man*).
- Explain that sometimes, whilst writing longer words, taking a break can help you to write more quickly and fluently because it provides an opportunity for the hand to move across the page.
- Read the words.
  Show Me Ask the children to write the words as quickly as possible.
- Children should compare their writing with their partner. Did they find it easy to write the words without taking a break?
  Get Up and Go Ask children to demonstrate the words on the OHT. Discuss the best place to take pen breaks in the words, and why.

abominable snowman

literature

disinterested

explanatory

memorable

OHT **8**

Independent work — using PCM for Unit 8

- Read the words aloud.
- The children should write the words, first without a pen break and then with one.
- Ask children to complete the evaluation.
- Children copy the pattern in the space at the bottom of the page.

Extra practice/Homework

- Children make up their own *supercalifragilisticexpialidocious* word. They try writing it out at speed without a break, then with a break. Which is easier?

9 Different styles for different purposes

Unit focus: fast and fluent writing, writing for note making and writing for presentation.
Spelling link: high-frequency words.

Whole-class session   using OHT 9

- Explain to the children that you don't always need to do your very best writing – it depends what the purpose of your writing is. If you're writing for a presentational purpose (e.g. a formal letter, a story, for homework) you need to use your best writing so that it is clear for everyone to read. If your writing is just for yourself, you can use 'fast and fluent' writing, which is fast, but still legible, although it doesn't need to be your neatest writing.
- If you need to make notes, you use 'note-making handwriting' – a rough style with abbreviations. Remind them that they already know a lot about abbreviations, as they use them whenever they send text messages.
- Read the words in the left-hand column, and look at how the first one is written in the various styles.

  Show Me Ask the children to write the rest of the words in each of the different styles.

- Children should compare their writing with their partner. Can they see the difference in the types of writing?

  Get Up and Go Ask children to demonstrate the words on the OHT.

Independent work   using PCM for Unit 9

- The children should write the invitation in fast and fluent handwriting and then in note-making handwriting.
- Ask children to complete the evaluation.
- Children copy the pattern in the space at the bottom of the page.

Extra practice/Homework

- Children write out their own party invitation in a neat hand. Then they copy it out in fast and fluent writing, and write the invitation in note form.

OHT **9**

Word	Notes	Fast & fluent	Presentation
without	w'out	without	without
birthday			
important			
something			
children			

10 Assessment

Unit focus: assessment and consolidation of writing at speed and developing style for speed.

NB: This unit serves as a consolidation of some of the work done in the first nine units and can be used as a checkpoint for children's progress.

Whole-class session   using OHT 10

- Read through the limerick.

  Show Me Children write the following words at speed to practise these things: joining from *t*: *packets*, *two*; optional joining from *g* and *y*: *grass*, *young*; joining from *f*: *farmer*, *from*; joining from *s*: *seeds*, *soon*, *pass*, *grass*, *sit*; joining from *w*: *was*, *swallowed*, *weeds*; joining from *v*: *covered*.

- Discuss any variations after each showing. Check that the joins are correctly formed and that the writing is legible.
- Have children made any pen breaks in the longer words? Revisit why this might be helpful at speed.
- Have a general discussion about slope.
- You can use the box on the OHT to model words or joins as appropriate, or to invite children to come up and demonstrate their writing.

Independent work   using PCM for Unit 10

- Children copy out the limerick at speed, taking note of the issues covered in the whole-class session.
- They then evaluate more fully each of the aspects listed.
- Children copy the pattern in the space at the bottom of the page.

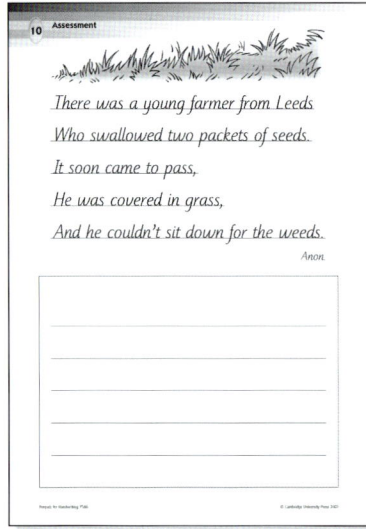

There was a young farmer from Leeds
Who swallowed two packets of seeds.
It soon came to pass,
He was covered in grass,
And he couldn't sit down for the weeds.
                                        Anon

OHT **10**

11 Haiku project: making notes

Unit focus: practising note-making handwriting.
Text link: to analyse poetic style and use of form; to make notes for different purposes.

Whole-class session — using OHT 11

- Introduce the whole haiku project. Over a number of sessions, the children will explore, plan, draft, redraft and publish a finished haiku of their own. At each stage of the process, appropriate handwriting skills will be developed.
- What do the children know about haiku? Discuss prior knowledge and, if necessary, remind them that haiku generally have 17 syllables arranged in three lines of 5, 7, 5 syllables.
- Introduce the OHT. Read both haiku and consider moods and feelings expressed in each.
- Discuss the 'Features of haiku' section, then relate them to the annotations on the first haiku.
- Agree together how to annotate the second haiku. Remind the children that they are making notes, so quick note-making handwriting is appropriate.

Independent work — using PCM for Unit 11

- Children should annotate at least two of the haiku on the page, considering form, language and mood. (The fourth haiku is by Basho, a haiku master, Japanese, 1644–1694. It is a translation, and does not have 17 syllables.)
- They should use note-making handwriting.

Extra practice/Homework

- Children research Basho or other haiku writers on the Internet, and make notes.

OHT **11**

12 Haiku project: organising ideas

Unit focus: practising fast and fluent handwriting.
Text link: to convey feelings or moods in a poem through careful selection of words; to make notes for different purposes.

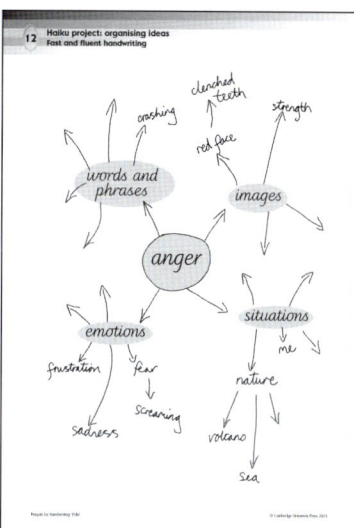

Whole-class session — using OHT 12

- In this session the children will collect ideas and images for developing a haiku of their own.
- Introduce the OHT. Explain the notion of a spider diagram as a way of organising ideas. Point out that it requires fast and fluent handwriting.
- Point out the central theme: anger.
- Point out the sub-themes: words and phrases, images, emotions, situations.
- Take each sub-theme in turn and explore the ideas.

  Get Up and Go Invite children to come up to complete the diagrams with ideas of their own, using appropriate handwriting.

Independent work — using PCM for Unit 12

- Children should select a theme of their choice and then build their own spider diagram.
- They should use fast and fluent handwriting.

Extra practice/Homework — using PCM for Unit 12

- Reissue the PCM for additional practice of writing fast and fluently whilst organising ideas.

OHT **12**

13 Haiku project: producing a draft

Unit focus: using fast and fluent writing to prepare a first draft and note-making handwriting to annotate it.
Text link: to convey feelings or moods in a poem through careful selection of words; to use abbreviations in note taking; to use structure of poems read as basis for own version.

Whole-class session using OHT 13

- In this session the children are going to be using the ideas and images collected during the previous session to develop a haiku of their own.
- Introduce the OHT and the notion of drawing ideas together and writing a first draft.
- Discuss the handwriting features of the two styles used on the page: note-making form for the ideas and fast and fluent for the first draft (see Unit 9 and Introduction page 15, if anyone's memory needs refreshing).

  Get Up and Go Invite children to contribute new ideas to either box.
  Show Me Ask the children to speed-write a phrase (e.g. *noisy seagulls screeching overhead*) in note form, including abbreviations and using quick joins only.

Independent work

- Children should begin to jot down ideas and write a first draft for a haiku based on their spider diagram.
- They should use note-making handwriting for recording initial ideas and fast and fluent handwriting for their draft.

Extra practice/Homework

- Children continue to work on their draft.

OHT **13**

14 Haiku project: publishing the haiku

Unit focus: practising presentation handwriting.
Text link: to convey feelings or moods in a poem through careful selection of words; to use structure of poems read as basis for own version.

Whole-class session using OHT 14

- In this session the children are going to be publishing their own haiku.
- Introduce the OHT. Discuss how the haiku has developed from the draft (OHT 13).
- Discuss the features of presentation that have been annotated.

  Get Up and Go Invite children to identify and annotate other key presentation features.

OHT **14**

Independent work

- Children should publish their haiku.
- They should use all the presentation features they identified on the OHT plus any others they feel are appropriate (e.g. colour for borders and illustrations).

Extra practice/Homework

- Children publish an alternative version of their haiku, varying the presentation features. The preferred version could then be mounted in a class book.

15 Haiku project: evaluation

Unit focus: evaluating handwriting within the haiku project.
Text link: to evaluate own work.

Whole-class session   using OHT 15

- In this session the children are going to be considering and evaluating the different handwriting styles used throughout the project.
- Introduce the OHT. Discuss the chart. The columns show different purposes for handwriting; the rows show different handwriting styles.
- Revisit OHTs 11–14 to remind the children of the different handwriting styles and purposes.
- Begin to fill in the chart on OHT 15, identifying the handwriting styles used at the different stages.
- Model how to complete the evaluation at the end of the chart, focusing on handwriting and presentation issues. What could have been done more effectively?

Independent work   using photocopy of OHT 15

- Provide each child with a photocopy of the OHT for each to evaluate his or her own project.
- The evaluation box at the bottom should include at least one feature that could have been improved.

Extra practice/Homework

- Children select another piece of published work from their books and evaluate its presentation using similar criteria.

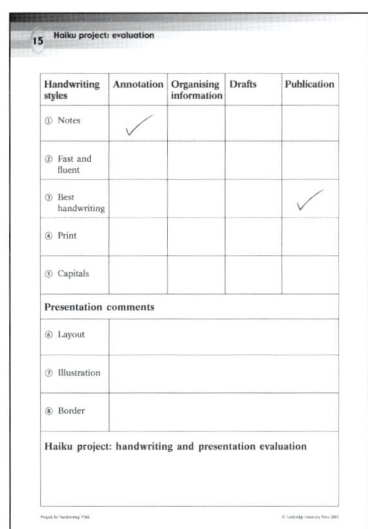

OHT **15**

16 Letter project: making notes

Unit focus: practising note-making handwriting.
Text link: to make notes for different purposes; to use simple abbreviations in note taking; to read other examples intended to inform, persuade; to fillet passages for relevant information; to construct an argument in note form to persuade others to a point of view.

NB: this project is scaffolded around a geography topic (QCA Geography Unit 12). You may prefer to substitute other topics for independent work.

Whole-class session   using OHT 16

- Introduce the whole letter project. Over a number of sessions, the children will explore, plan, draft and publish a letter to the local paper offering opinions.
- Introduce the OHT. Explain that this is an extract from a longer newspaper article about whether the High Street should be pedestrianised. Read the extract together.
- Discuss how making notes and annotating the text can be used to gather information. Read the note-form annotations and discuss the features.
  Get Up and Go Invite children to add more annotations on either side of the argument.
  Show Me In pairs, children write a further argument of their own in note form. Share and discuss.

Independent work   using PCM for Unit 16

- Children should annotate the whole newspaper article as demonstrated in the whole-class session, or make notes for their own project.
- They should use note-making handwriting.

Extra practice/Homework

- Children note down further points both for and against to contribute to the next handwriting session.

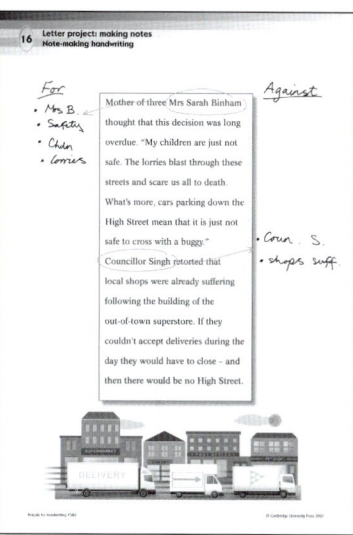

OHT **16**

Unit focus: practising note-making handwriting.

Text link: to make notes for different purposes; to use simple abbreviations in note taking; to construct an argument in note form to persuade others to a point of view.

Whole-class session using OHT 17

- The children will need the notes they made on the OHT in the previous session as well as ideas from homework activities.
- Introduce the OHT. Explain that it is a writing frame for structuring an argument. Ask the children what kind of writing they think would be most appropriate for this purpose.
- Note that this argument is in favour of closing the High Street to traffic. Discuss what is meant by the abbreviations and notes already filled in.

  Get Up and Go Invite children to add more notes to the boxes, following the structure given.

Independent work using PCM for Unit 17

- Children should begin to scaffold an argument in favour of NOT closing the High Street to traffic (or another issue if appropriate).
- They should use note-making handwriting.

Extra practice/Homework using PCM for Unit 17

- Children use a copy of the scaffolding frame on PCM 17 to draft initial thoughts on another issue (e.g. should they have homework, should they go to school on a Saturday). They should use a note-making handwriting style.

OHT **17**

Unit focus: using fast and fluent handwriting to produce a draft; using note-making handwriting to annotate a draft.

Text link: to make notes for different purposes; to present effectively grouped and linked information; to draft letters for real purposes; to construct an argument in full text form to persuade others to a point of view.

Whole-class session using OHT 18

- Revisit the scaffolding notes from OHT 17, supporting the closing of the High Street to traffic.
- Introduce OHT 18. Explain that the scaffolding frame has been used to write a draft letter to the editor of the local paper. Read the letter together.
- Consider how the letter is set out and how the language is used to gain attention and present the argument to the reader.
- Identify any errors (spelling and punctuation).
- Discuss the improvements already noted. Then continue to annotate, correct and improve the letter.
- A note-making style of handwriting should be used.

Independent work

- Children should draft a letter arguing that the High Street should not be closed to traffic (or based on another issue if appropriate).
- They should use fast and fluent handwriting for the draft.

Extra practice/Homework

- Children begin to edit their letter to annotate, correct and improve it, using a note-making handwriting style. They shouldn't produce a final version yet.

OHT **18**

19 Letter project: publishing a letter

Unit focus: practising presentation handwriting.
Text link: to find information and present information that is effectively grouped and linked; to write letters for real purposes; to construct an argument in full text form to persuade others to a point of view.

Whole-class session   using OHT 19

- In this session the children are going to be publishing the final draft of their letter.
- Introduce the OHT. Discuss how the letter has developed from the draft letter on OHT 18.
- Discuss the features of the letter that have been annotated.

  Get Up and Go Invite children to identify and annotate other key presentation features (e.g. date, underlining of focus, paragraph indents).
- Discuss how you might end the letter.

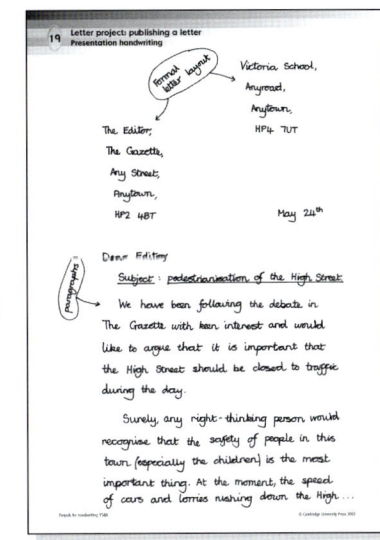

OHT **19**

Independent work

- Children should publish their own letter arguing that the High Street should not be closed to traffic (or another topic if appropriate).
- They should use all the presentation features they identified on the OHT plus any others that they think appropriate.
- Best handwriting should be used for this published version.

Extra practice/Homework

- Children research other styles of business letters using ICT or junk mail.

20 Letter project: evaluation

Unit focus: evaluating different handwriting styles used throughout the project.
Text link: to evaluate own work.

Whole-class session   using OHT 20

- In this session the children are going to be considering and evaluating the different handwriting styles used throughout the project.
- Introduce the OHT. Discuss the chart. The columns show different purposes for handwriting; the rows show different handwriting styles.
- Revisit OHTs 16–19 to remind the children of the different handwriting styles and purposes.
- Using OHT 20, begin to fill in the chart, identifying the handwriting styles used at the different stages.
- Model how to complete the evaluation at the end of the chart, focusing on handwriting and presentation issues. What could have been done more effectively?

OHT **20**

Independent work   using photocopy of OHT 20

- Provide each child with a copy of the OHT for each to evaluate his or her own project.
- The evaluation box at the bottom should include at least one feature that could have been improved.

Extra practice/Homework

- Children select another piece of published work from their books and evaluate its presentation using similar criteria.

21 Self-assessment: evaluating handwriting

Unit focus: evaluating own handwriting styles.
Text link: to evaluate own work.

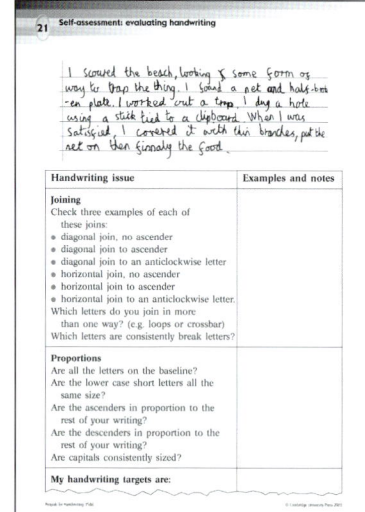

OHT **21**

Whole-class session   using OHT 21

- In this session the children will be evaluating the different handwriting styles they used throughout a project.
- Introduce the OHT. Discuss the sample writing and the chart extract.
- Begin to fill in the chart, identifying handwriting issues from the sample.
- Model how to complete the assessment form on PCM 21 and discuss how the author of this piece of writing should fill in the target-setting box at the end of the PCM.

Independent work   using PCM for Unit 21

- Children should complete the self-assessment sheet using a sample of recently completed writing.
- The target-setting box at the bottom should include at least two features that could be improved.

Extra practice/Homework

- Children select another piece of work to see if their handwriting is consistent.

22 Self-assessment: checking the joins

Unit focus: checking the joins in own handwriting.
Spelling link: word roots, prefixes, suffixes.

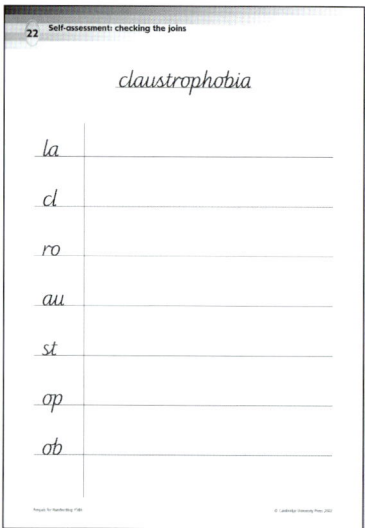

OHT **22**

Whole-class session   using OHT 22

- Talk about the word *claustrophobia*. Identify the joins used in it. Are the children confident using each join (particularly those to anticlockwise letters)?
- For each letter pattern shown in the column on the left, think of a word that uses that pattern.

  Get Up and Go Invite children to write the words on the lines. The class can discuss whether all the joins are correctly formed.
  Show Me Ask all children to write the words. Ask them to evaluate their writing each time.

Independent work   using PCM for Unit 22

- Agree what the words in Set C should be (e.g. *autograph, television, microscope, aquaplane, transport, auditorium, prehistoric*) before the children write them.
- Ask children to complete the evaluation.
- Children copy the pattern in the space at the bottom of the page.

Extra practice/Homework   using photocopy of OHT 22

- Children write their own words using each of the letter patterns shown on the OHT.
- Children find a familiar joke or poem and copy it out, focusing on joining correctly.

23 Self-assessment: consistency of size

Unit focus: checking own handwriting for consistency of size.
Vocabulary link: to extend vocabulary through puns.

Whole-class session — using OHT 23

- Compare the two versions of the joke on the OHT. What's the difference between them?

  Get Up and Go Invite children to ring inconsistently sized letters in the second version and ask them to explain what is wrong with the letter each time.

  Show Me Ask all children to write each of the words containing a ringed letter. Are their letters consistently sized? Focus their attention particularly on letters *e*, *f* and *s*, which are most commonly inconsistent. Ask the children to evaluate their writing each time.

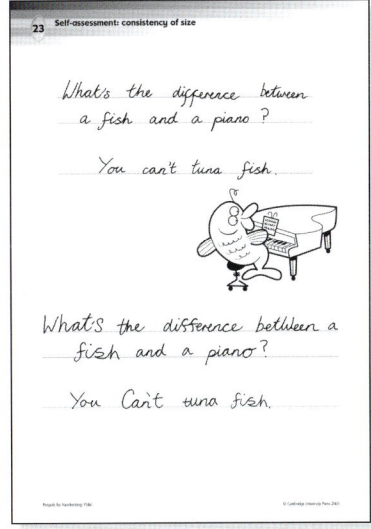

OHT 23

Independent work — using PCM for Unit 23

- Ask children to copy the menu carefully, focusing on consistency of size of all letters, including capitals.
- Can they think of any more items to add to the menu? They can write these on the back of the sheet.
- Ask children to complete the evaluation.
- Children copy the pattern in the space at the bottom of the page.

Extra practice/Homework — using photocopy of OHT 23

- Children copy the joke for themselves.
- Children find a familiar joke or poem and copy it out, focusing on maintaining consistency of letter size.

24 Self-assessment: letters resting on baseline

Unit focus: assessing position of letters relative to baseline in own writing.
Vocabulary link: to collect definitions of technical terms.

Whole-class session — using OHT 24

- Talk about the handwritten words on the OHT. Why does it matter that the letters do not all rest on the baseline?

  Get Up and Go Invite children to write each of the words on the OHT onto one of the lines on the pitch, using joined writing. Let the others discuss whether the letters are correctly aligned.

  Show Me Ask all children to try writing the words (drawing baselines if necessary). Ask the children to evaluate their writing each time.

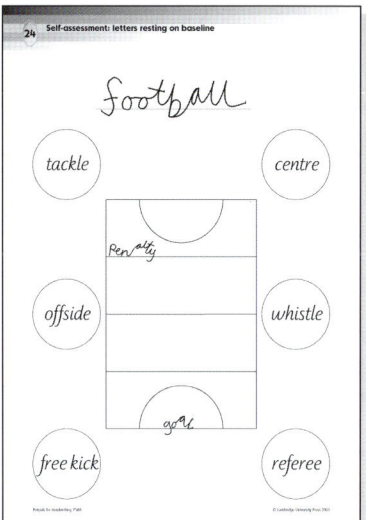

OHT 24

Independent work — using PCM for Unit 24

- Read the tips for serving in tennis.
- In the space provided, the children should copy the tips, focusing on keeping their letters on the baseline. Children who write on a slope may benefit from using the guidelines provided on page 64.
- Ask children to complete the evaluation.
- If there is time, children copy the pattern in the space at the bottom of the page.

Extra practice/Homework — using photocopy of OHT 24

- Ask the children to write their own definitions for some words to do with their favourite sport.
- Children can write footballing words in relevant places on the pitch shown on the OHT. They should draw baselines when necessary.
- Ask children to draw a 'pitch' for an alternative sporting event (e.g. netball, hockey, rounders, swimming, athletics) and write related words on the 'pitch'.

25 Self-assessment: ascenders and descenders

Unit focus: checking angle and length of ascenders and descenders in own writing.

Spelling link: meanings and spellings of connectives.

Whole-class session — using OHT 25

- Discuss what is wrong with each of the words written on the OHT. For example: are the ascenders and descenders parallel; is their height or length appropriate; are they consistently sized?

  Get Up and Go Invite children to explain what is wrong each time and to write a more acceptable version in the right-hand box.

  Show Me Ask all children to write each of the words. They should draw baselines if necessary. Focus their attention particularly on ascenders and descenders. Ask the children to evaluate their writing each time.

Independent work — using PCM for Unit 25

- Ask children to copy the passage carefully, focusing on ascenders and descenders.
- Ask children to complete the evaluation.
- Children copy the pattern in the space at the bottom of the page.

Extra practice/Homework — using PCM for Unit 25

- Children write a similar passage about poodles or another pet, using connectives.

26 Self-assessment: consistency of size of capitals and ascenders

Unit focus: checking consistency of size of capitals and ascenders in own writing.

Text link: layout of titles.

Whole-class session — using OHT 26

- Look at the book title on the OHT. Discuss the fact that the capital letters and the ascenders are all a consistent size (except lower case *t*, which is slightly shorter).

  Get Up and Go Invite children to copy the title, and/or to write up other book titles that they know. The class can evaluate the evenness of the offerings, drawing guidelines over the writing if desired.

  Show Me Ask all children to write the title. They should draw baselines if necessary. Focus their attention particularly on the consistency of size of the capitals and ascenders. Ask the children to evaluate their writing each time.

Independent work — using PCM for Unit 26

- Ask children to write the address carefully, focusing on layout and consistency of size of capitals and ascenders.
- Ask children to complete the evaluation.
- Children copy the pattern in the space at the bottom of the page.

Extra practice/Homework — using photocopy of OHT 26

- Children complete the OHT activity from the class session working independently and supplying their own book titles.

27 Writing at speed: inappropriate closing of letters

Unit focus: ensuring that letters are not closed inappropriately when writing at speed.

Text link: to recognise how poets manipulate words.

Whole-class session   using OHT 27

- Ask the children to identify each of the letters in the box. Explain that these are *u, y, h, s* written at speed by someone with bad handwriting! Ask children to explain what has happened to all of these letters.

  Get Up and Go Ask children to copy each of the words, writing as quickly as possible in joined writing. Ask the class to assess whether there are any letters closed which should remain open.

  Show Me Ask all children to write each of the words at speed. Ask the children to evaluate their writing each time.

Independent work   using PCM for Unit 27

- Ask children to copy the limerick in two minutes or less.
- They should complete the evaluation.
- Children copy the pattern in the space at the bottom of the page.

Extra practice/Homework

- Ask children to find and copy another limerick in fast and fluent writing. Can they time themselves to find out how long it takes to write it?

OHT 27

28 Writing at speed: identifying unclosed letters

Unit focus: ensuring that letters are not left open inappropriately when writing at speed.

Spelling link: word origins and derivations.

Whole-class session   using OHT 28

- Ask the children to identify each of the letters in the box. Explain that these are *a, d, e, g, o* written at speed by someone with bad handwriting! Ask children to explain what has happened to all of these letters.

- Do any of the children recognise the words as musical terms? Do they know what each one means? (*adagio = slow; allegro = fast; allegretto = 'little allegro' = quite fast; vivace = lively and fast*)

  Get Up and Go Ask children to copy each of the words, writing as quickly as possible. Ask the class to assess whether any of the letters are not properly closed.

  Show Me Ask all children to write each of the words at speed. Ask the children to evaluate their writing each time.

Independent work   using PCM for Unit 28

- Discuss which section of the orchestra each instrument belongs in. If necessary, the children can note *s* (strings), *w* (woodwind), *b* (brass) or *p* (percussion) beside instrument names.

- Give children two minutes to complete the activity. They should then complete the evaluation.

- Children copy the pattern in the space at the bottom of the page.

Extra practice/Homework

- Ask children to find and copy six other words in fast and fluent writing to describe different styles of familiar music. Can they time themselves to find out how long it takes to write the words?

OHT 28

Unit focus: assessing spacing within words when writing at speed.

Spelling link: word roots and prefixes.

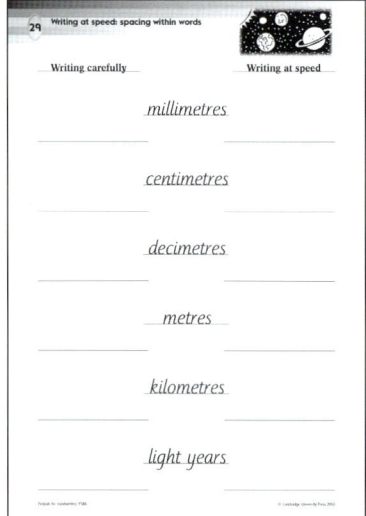

OHT 29

Whole-class session   using OHT 29

- Can the children tell you what all these words have in common?

  Get Up and Go Ask children to copy each of the words twice, first writing carefully, then writing as quickly as possible. Is the spacing within the words consistent both times?

  Show Me Ask all children to write each of the words, both carefully and at speed. Discuss what happens to spaces within words when writing at speed. Ask the children to evaluate their writing each time.

Independent work   using PCM for Unit 29

- Read the problem about measuring together. (**NB:** the answers are 1082 and 918 millilitres.)
- Give the children two minutes to copy as much of the problem as they can.
- Children should complete the evaluation.
- Children copy the pattern in the space at the bottom of the page.

Extra practice/Homework

- Children write out their own mathematical problem for a friend to solve.
- Ask children to find and copy six other words that are measures of time. They should write each word first carefully then quickly, and then check for consistent spacing within the words each time.

Unit focus: assessing spacing between words when writing at speed.

Spelling link: critical features of words.

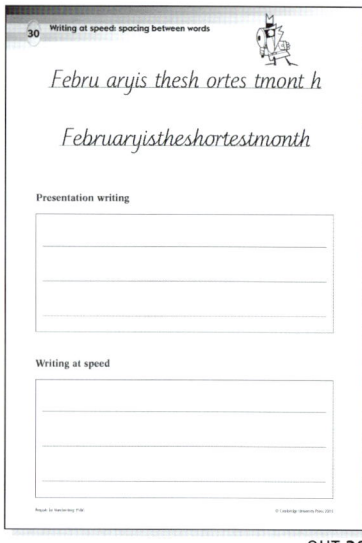

OHT 30

Whole-class session   using OHT 30

- Cover up the OHT except for the first line of writing. Can the children read what it says? (*February is the shortest month.*) Then show them the second line of writing. Discuss how spaces between words are important in order that readers can read efficiently!

  Get Up and Go Ask children to copy the text – using correct spacing – in each of the boxes using the type of writing described. What is the effect of writing at speed on spacing between words?

  Show Me Ask all children to write the phrase both carefully and at speed. Discuss what happens to spaces between words when writing at speed. Ask the children to evaluate their writing each time.

Independent work   using PCM for Unit 30

- Read the jokes together.
- Give the children two minutes to copy as much of the text as they can.
- Children should complete the evaluation.
- Children copy the pattern in the space at the bottom of the page.

Extra practice/Homework

- Ask children to write out the months of the year in a continuous list both in their best writing and as quickly as they can. They should assess the spacing between words in each case.

31 Playscript project: collecting information

Unit focus: using note-making handwriting when collecting information.

Text link: to annotate passages in detail in response to specific questions.

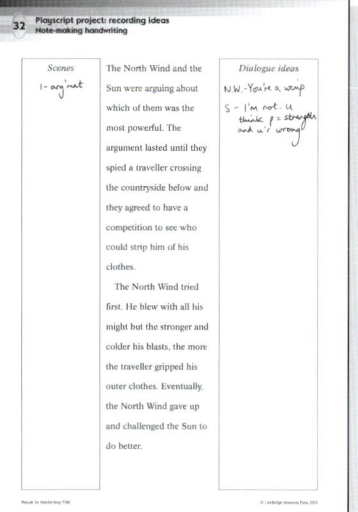

OHT **31**

Whole-class session   using OHT 31

- Introduce the whole playscript project. Over a number of sessions, the children will explore, plan, draft, redraft and publish a finished playscript of their own. At each stage of the process, appropriate handwriting skills will be developed.
- Read the beginning of the fable on OHT 31 together and discuss the character of the North Wind. Ask children to underline evidence in the text to support their ideas. As they do so, begin to use notes to record the ideas. Do the children agree with the annotations already marked? If so, they can add to them, otherwise they should change them.
- Repeat the process for the Sun.
- Remind the children that they are making notes, so quick note-making handwriting is appropriate.

Independent work   using PCM for Unit 31

- Children should annotate the rest of the fable, making character notes about the Sun and confirming or adapting their ideas about the North Wind.
- They should use note-making handwriting.

Extra practice/Homework

- Children make notes to begin to explore what the traveller might have been thinking.

32 Playscript project: recording ideas

Unit focus: using note-making handwriting to record ideas when planning a piece of writing.

Text link: to annotate passages in detail in response to specific questions.

OHT **32**

Whole-class session   using OHT 32

- Remind the children of the way you characterised the North Wind and the Sun in the previous session. How might they talk? What kind of language would they use? What might they say?
- Note down children's ideas in the 'Dialogue ideas' box, modelling how to scribe and edit using note-making handwriting.

  Show Me Let children work in pairs to note down some sample dialogue.

- Ask them to think about how they would divide this passage into scenes for a play. In the 'Scenes' box, jot down the scenes they think they would use.
- Remind the children that they are making notes, so quick note-making handwriting is appropriate.

Independent work using PCM for Unit 32

- Children should work in pairs/threes, starting at the beginning of the text again in order to allow each group to put their own interpretation on the play. They should think about scenes and dialogue between the North Wind and the Sun and make notes in the appropriate column.
- They should use note-making handwriting.

Extra practice/Homework

- Children make notes to begin to explore what the traveller might have been saying to himself.

33 Playscript project: producing a draft

Unit focus: using fast and fluent handwriting to produce a draft and note-making handwriting to annotate it.

Text link: to prepare a short section of story as a script using stage directions, setting, etc.

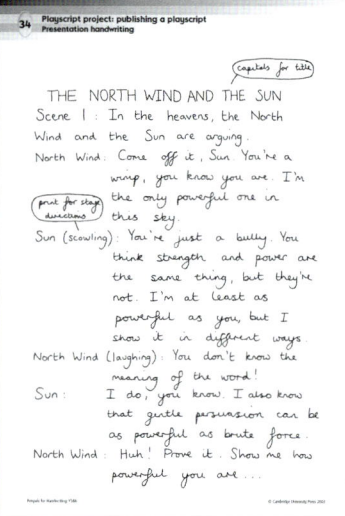

OHT **33**

Whole-class session   using OHT 33

- In this session children will be using the dialogue notes they made during the previous session as the basis for writing and annotating a draft of their playscript.

- Discuss the OHT. First read through the original draft – written in fast and fluent handwriting – then discuss the notes and annotations (written in note-making handwriting). Do the children think they can improve the draft? Can the children suggest any other improvements? Edit the text appropriately.

- Discuss why the draft is in fast and fluent handwriting but the notes aren't.

- Remind the children that they should use appropriate handwriting forms for the different purposes while they work on their playscripts.

Independent work

- Children can continue to work in their groups from the previous session to write a first draft. If time is short, you may want to ask different sets of children to work on different scenes of the story.

- They should use fast and fluent handwriting for the first draft and note-making handwriting for additional annotations.

Extra practice/Homework

- Children read their draft playscripts out loud to see if the language flows and sounds appropriate. Remind them to record edits using note-making handwriting.

34 Playscript project: publishing a playscript

Unit focus: using presentation writing to publish a playscript.

Text link: to prepare a short section of story as a script using stage directions, setting, etc.

OHT **34**

Whole-class session   using OHT 34

- In this session children will be publishing their playscripts for children in another group to present. This means that the writing and presentation must be to a high standard in order that the actors can read their scripts. Stage directions must also be clear.

- Introduce the OHT. Discuss how the playscript has developed from the draft on OHT 33.

- Discuss the features of the playscript that have been annotated.

   Get Up and Go Invite children to identify and annotate other key features of presentation (e.g. print for scene setting and indentations).

Independent work

- Children should publish their own playscript. Each child in the group will need to make a copy so that each actor will have a script.

- They should use all the presentation features they identified on the OHT plus any others they feel appropriate.

- Best handwriting should be used for this published version.

Extra practice/Homework

- Ask children to explore the different layout conventions for playscripts used in different editions of plays.

35 Playscript project: evaluation

Unit focus: evaluating the different styles of writing used in the playscript project.

Text link: to prepare a short section of story as a script using stage direction, setting, etc.

Whole-class session using OHT 35

- In this session children are going to be considering and evaluating the different handwriting styles used throughout the project.
- Introduce the OHT. Discuss the chart. The columns show different purposes for handwriting; the rows show different handwriting styles.
- Revisit OHTs 30–34 to remind the children of the different handwriting styles and purposes.
- Begin to fill in the chart on the OHT, identifying the handwriting styles used at the different stages.
- Model how to complete the evaluation at the end of the chart, focusing on handwriting and presentation issues. What could have been done more effectively?

Independent work using photocopy of OHT 35

- Provide each child with a copy of the OHT for each to evaluate his or her own project.
- The evaluation box at the bottom should include at least one feature that could have been improved.

Extra practice/Homework

- Give the children time during the week to lay out part of their script on the computer, exploring layout, fonts available, etc. Then ask them to write a brief evaluation of the differences between handwritten scripts and computer printouts.

OHT **35**

36 Information notice project: collecting and organising information

Unit focus: using note-making handwriting to collect information.

Text link: to read and understand examples of official language.

NB: this project is scaffolded around a notice advocating safe Internet use (QCA ICT Unit 6d). You may prefer to substitute other topics for independent work.

Whole-class session using OHT 36

- Introduce the whole information notice project. Over a number of sessions, the children will explore, plan, draft, redraft and publish a finished public information notice. At each stage of the process, appropriate handwriting skills will be developed.
- Read the extracts on the OHT from a school's Internet access and information ethics policy (or make extracts from your own school's policy). Explain that the purpose of this official document is to make the school's position clear to parents, staff, governors and inspectors. Discuss any unfamiliar formal language and jot down definitions on the OHT.

  Show Me Ask children to summarise what they think are the most important points.
- Remind the children that quick note-making handwriting is appropriate.

Independent work using PCM for Unit 36

- Tell the children that over the next few sessions they are going to make a notice for display to remind users how to make responsible use of the computers. They will need to include some information about the Internet and e-mail, but other issues could also be included.
- Ask them to select information for inclusion in their notices by annotating, crossing out or adding to information on the PCM.
- They should use note-making handwriting.

Extra practice/Homework

- Children consider how this information could be adapted for home use and make notes.

OHT **36**

Unit focus: using note-making handwriting when planning a text.

Text link: to develop a journalistic style of writing through considering what is of public interest, and the selection and presentation of information.

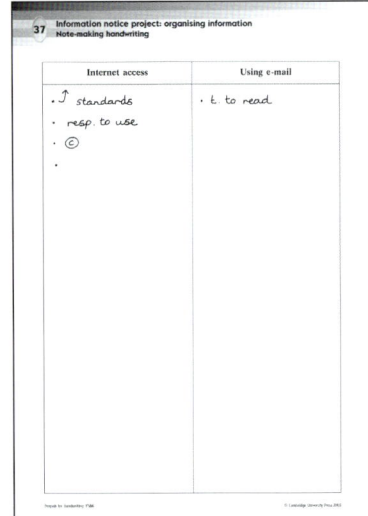

OHT 37

Whole-class session   using OHT 37

- In the session the children will combine information they selected in the previous session with new information, and organise it under headings. The children will need the policy document they annotated from the previous session (PCM 36).

- Look at the information already noted on the OHT. Do the children agree that these are important points? Which additional points do the children think it is important for pupils to be aware of?

  Get Up and Go Let some children add annotations to the sheet.

  Show Me Children can explore ways of making notes for agreed points. Emphasise the fact that note making is personal – it is important that the note maker can interpret the notes at a later date, but it is less important that others can interpret the notes.

- Remind the children that they are making notes, so quick note-making handwriting is appropriate.

Independent work   using PCM for Unit 37

- Children should work in pairs, continuing to add information and ideas, sorting into the appropriate column. Remind them that the audience for the notice is primarily their peers, so they should select information appropriately.

- They should use note-making handwriting.

Extra practice/Homework

- Ask children to find examples of consumer information notices to give ideas on layout, etc.

Unit focus: using fast and fluent handwriting to produce a draft and note-making handwriting to improve it.

Text link: to secure control of impersonal writing; to select the appropriate style and form to suit a specific purpose and audience.

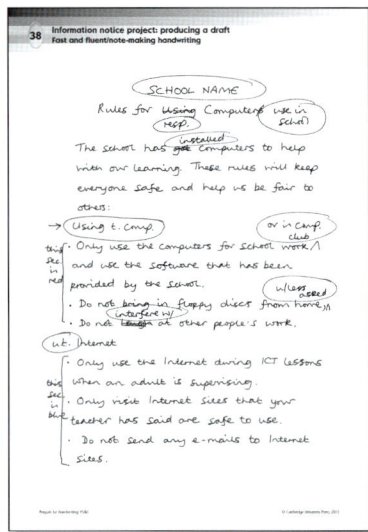

OHT 38

Whole-class session   using OHT 38

- In this session children will be using the notes they made during the previous session as the basis of writing and annotating a draft of their notice.

- Discuss the OHT. First read through the original draft – written in fast and fluent handwriting – then discuss the notes and annotations. Do the children think they can improve the draft? Can the children suggest any other improvements? Is there other information they think should be included/excluded? Edit the text appropriately.

- Remind children about layout and audience.

- Discuss why the draft is in fast and fluent handwriting and the notes are in note-making handwriting.

- Remind the children that they should use appropriate handwriting forms for the different purposes while they work on their notice.

Independent work

- Children should begin to draft their notices. Remind them about use of colour – which can't be shown on a black and white OHT!

- They should use fast and fluent handwriting for the first draft and note-making handwriting for additional annotations.

Extra practice/Homework

- Ask children to plan an alternative design, either by hand or using a computer if they have access to one.

Unit focus: using presentation handwriting to publish an information notice.

Text link: to secure control of impersonal writing; to select the appropriate style and form to suit a specific purpose and audience.

Whole-class session using OHT 39

- In this session children will be publishing their notices. You could ask an impartial judge to select one to place near each computer. The presentation and layout must be to a high standard in order that other computer users will be able to read and understand them.
- Introduce the OHT. Discuss how the notice has developed from the draft on OHT 38.
- Discuss the features of the notice that have been annotated.

  Get Up and Go Invite the children to identify and annotate other key features of presentation.

Independent work

- Children should publish their own notice.
- They should use all the presentation features they identified on the OHT plus any others they think appropriate.
- Print script should be used for this published version because it is generally legible from a greater distance.

Extra practice/Homework

- Children produce an alternative version of their notice using coloured pens or ICT.

OHT **39**

Unit focus: evaluating the different styles of writing used in the information notice project.

Text link: to comment critically on language, style and success of non-fiction texts such as reports, leaflets.

Whole-class session using OHT 40

- In this session the children are going to be considering and evaluating the different handwriting styles used throughout the project.
- Introduce the OHT. Discuss the chart. The columns show different purposes for handwriting; the rows show different handwriting styles.
- Revisit OHTs 36–39 to remind the children of the different handwriting styles and purposes.
- Begin to fill in the chart, identifying the handwriting styles used at the different stages.
- Model how to complete the evaluation at the end of the chart, focusing on handwriting and presentation issues. What could have been done more effectively?

Independent work using photocopy of OHT 40

- Provide each child with a copy of the OHT for each to evaluate his or her own project.
- The evaluation box at the bottom should include at least one feature that could have been improved.

Extra practice/Homework

- Ask children to add a brief evaluation comparing the notice they made in school with the one they made at home.

OHT **40**

Ha Ha!

"Who's that tickling my back?"
said the wall.
"Me," said the little caterpillar,
"I'm learning to crawl."

Anon.

Write the rhyme, thinking about the slope.

Evaluation

Name

Date

The Crocodile

If you should meet a crocodile
Don't take a stick and poke him;
Ignore the welcome in his smile,
Be careful not to stroke him.
For as he sleeps upon the Nile
He thinner gets and thinner;
And when'er you meet a crocodile
He's ready for his dinner.

Anon.

Write the rhyme in joined writing.

_____

_____

_____

_____

_____

_____

_____

Evaluation

Circle any joins that you need to practise.

Name

Date

Batty Betty

Batty Betty bought some butter.
"This butter's bitter," she told her brother.
"Bottled butter tastes less bitter,
Let's boil the butter to make it better."
Anon.

Write the tongue-twister at speed in joined writing.

Evaluation

How did you join the *t*s?

Other comments:

© Gill Budgell (Frattempo) and Kate Ruttle 2009

Name .... Date ....

The Old Grey Donkey

Donkey, Donkey, old and grey,
Open your jaw and gently bray;
Lift your ears and blow your horn,
To wake the world this joyful morn.

Write the rhyme at speed in joined writing.

_____

_____

_____

_____

Evaluation

Did you join from *g, y, j*?

Other comments:

Name   Date

Q: _What do you call the flour that fairies make bread with?_

A: _Elf-raising flour!_

FLOUR

Write the joke at speed in joined writing.

Evaluation
How did you join from _f_?
Other comments:

Name

Date

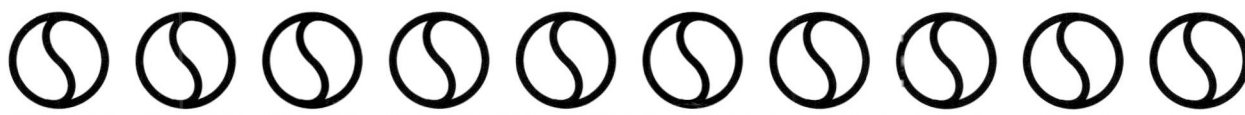

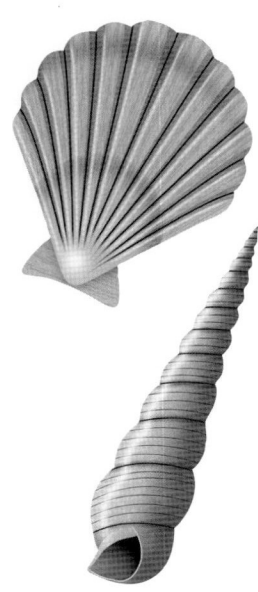

Seashells

She sells seashells on the seashore:
Seashells in sandwiches,
Seashells with stars;
She even sells seashells in shiny glass jars.
Anon.

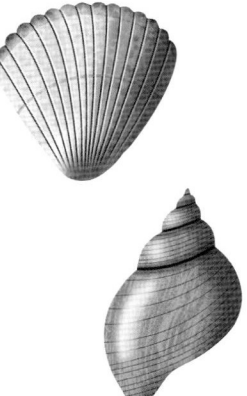

Write the tongue-twister at speed in joined writing.

_____

_____

_____

_____

Evaluation

How did you join from *s*?

Other comments:

Name _____ Date _____

matzo's menu

amazing pizzas
volcanic ravioli
awesome kiwis

~

examined and boxed
for your convenience

Write the menu at speed in joined writing.

_____

_____

_____

_____

_____

_____

Evaluation

Did you join from *x* and *z*?

How did you form *v* and *w*?

Other comments:

Name .... Date ....

supercalifragilisticexpialidocious

antidisestablishmentarianism

Write the words with no breaks.

_____

_____

Write the words with breaks.

_____

_____

Evaluation

Did you prefer using pen breaks? Why?

Other comments:

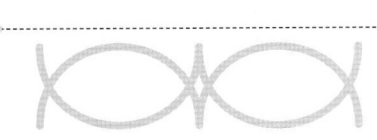

Name

Date

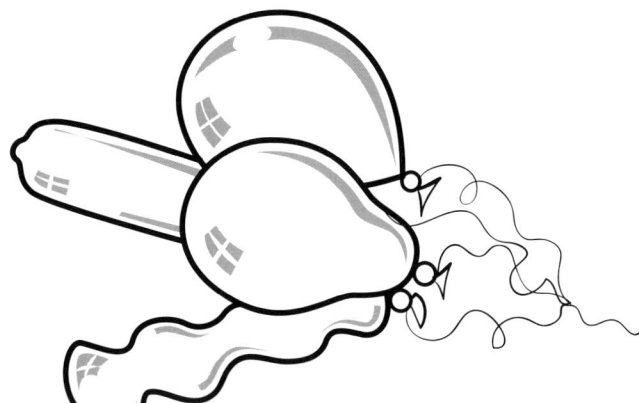

Dear Friend,

Please come to my party

on Saturday 28th August at half

past seven at Saint Benedict's Hall.

Please reply as soon as possible.

From Matthew

Copy the invitation in fast and fluent writing.

Write the invitation in note form.

Evaluation

Name .... Date ....

ele ele ele ele ele ele ele

There was a young farmer from Leeds
Who swallowed two packets of seeds.
It soon came to pass,
He was covered in grass,
And he couldn't sit down for the weeds.

Anon.

Write the limerick at speed in joined writing.

_____

_____

_____

_____

Evaluation

Comment on the following:
- slope
- joins from   t   f
                  y   s
                  g   x
- breaks.

Other comments:

ele

Name .... Date ....

Make notes about two of the haiku.

Forever friendly.
Many people but one mind.
Chatty, laughing times.

Run, tackle, away:
Body machine pumping hard.
Goal! Moment of joy.

Dazzling white snowflakes:
Watching from bedroom darkness,
Comforting hot drink.

Translated from Japanese (not 17 syllables)

Waterjar cracks:
I lie awake
This icy night.

Basho

Name

Date

Organise ideas for your own haiku using fast and fluent writing.

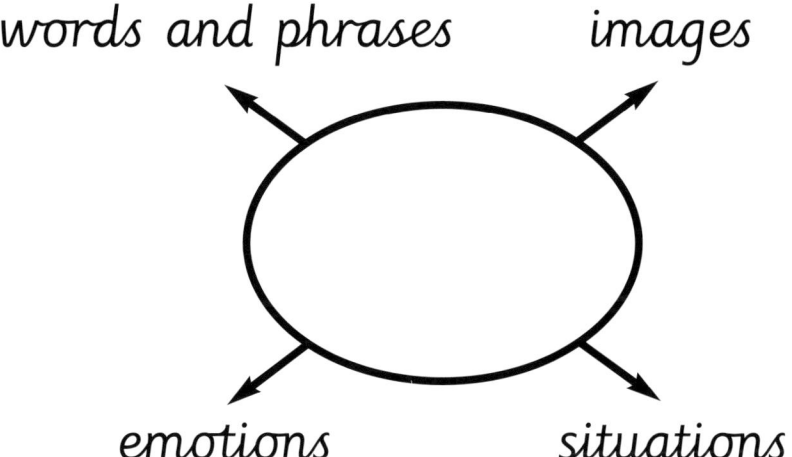

Make notes on the article.

HIGH STREET TO BECOME PEDESTRIAN PRECINCT?

By Gill Budgell and Kate Ruttle

At a council meeting held last night in the Town Hall, a heated discussion took place between councillors and local residents. The issue was whether we should pedestrianise our High Street and ban all vehicles from entering during the day. Mother of three Mrs Sarah Binham thought that this decision was long overdue. "My children are just not safe. The lorries blast through these streets and scare us all to death. What's more, cars parking down the High Street mean that it is just not safe to cross with a buggy."

Councillor Singh retorted that local shops were already suffering following the building of the out-of-town superstore and if they couldn't accept deliveries during the day they would have to close – and then there would be no High Street. Delivery driver Mark Densham added, "Pedestrian barriers should be erected to keep the pedestrians on the pavement where they belong. I waste too much time dodging pedestrians and time is money for me."

At this point, Mrs Sarah Binham left the meeting in disgust, saying, "I don't believe what this town is coming to. Nobody cares about the safety of our children." The debate continues. If you have any opinions please phone our customer line on 01234 5678910.

Name

Date

Use note-making handwriting to record your ideas.

Paragraph 1: State point of view	
Paragraph 2: Main supporting argument	
Paragraph 3: Main counter argument plus reasons for disagreeing	
Paragraph 4: Additional supporting arguments plus conclusion	

Name

Date

Use one of the handwriting projects and complete the following sheet as honestly as you can.

Handwriting issue	Examples and notes
Letter formation Are all your letters formed correctly? Which letters do you form in more than one way? Are any letters closed that should be open? Are any letters open that should be closed?	
Joining Check three examples of each of these joins: ● diagonal join, no ascender ● diagonal join to ascender ● diagonal join to an anticlockwise letter ● horizontal join, no ascender ● horizontal join to ascender ● horizontal join to an anticlockwise letter. Which letters do you join in more than one way? Which letters are consistently break letters?	
Proportions Are all the letters on the baseline? Are the lower case short letters all the same size? Are the ascenders in proportion to the rest of your writing? Are the descenders in proportion to the rest of your writing? Are capitals consistently sized?	
Spacing Are spaces within words consistent? Are letters too close together or too far apart? Are pen breaks used appropriately in longer words? Are spaces between words consistent? Are words too close together or too far apart?	
Style and presentation Are you using different styles of handwriting for different purposes? ● Note making ● Fast and fluent ● Best handwriting ● Print ● Capitals ● Interesting lettering and decoration	
My handwriting targets are:	

Name .... Date ....

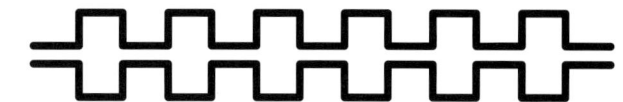

Combine parts of words from Set A and Set B. Write the new words in joined writing in Set C.

Set A	Set B	Set C
auto	scope	
tele	plane	
micro	vision	
aqua	graph	
trans	port	
audi	historic	
pre	torium	

Evaluation

Check the anticlockwise joins (joins to *a, c, d, g, o, q, s*). Are they all formed correctly?

Check joins to ascenders (*h, l, t*). Are they formed correctly?

Other comments:

Name .... Date ....

Menu

Fishy flakes

Crispy cod

Scottish salmon

Baked sea bass

Stuffed Suffolk lobster

Dressed Norfolk crab

Whelks, prawns and shrimps

Copy the menu carefully. Use joined handwriting.

_____

_____

_____

_____

_____

_____

_____

Evaluation

Are the lower case short letters all the same size (including _s_ and _w_)?

Are ascenders and descenders in proportion to the rest of the writing (including f)?

Other comments:

Name .... Date ....

Copy the tips for serving. Use joined handwriting.
Make sure your letters rest on the baseline.

Tips for serving in tennis

1   Don't throw the ball up too high.

2   Try to throw the ball up straight.

3   Aim to hit the ball with the

centre of your racket.

Evaluation

Are all the letters resting on the line?   Other comments:
Are all descenders a consistent length?

Name .... Date ....

Copy the passage in joined writing.

Although the Dalmatian is quite a large breed of dog, wolfhounds are bigger. They are often quite friendly towards little children and consequently they can make good family pets.

Evaluation

Are ascenders and descenders in proportion to the rest of your writing?

Are all ascenders parallel?

Are all descenders parallel?

Other comments:

Name .... Date ....

Read the address.

Copy the address in joined writing.

Miss Fiona Walker

57 Forrest Street

Killicrankie

Scotland

_PE32 4RW_

Evaluation

Are capitals consistently sized?

Are capitals the same height as ascenders?

Other comments:

Name ....   Date ....

A dentist named Archibald Moss

Fell in love with the dainty Miss Ross.

Since he held in abhorrence

Her given name, Florence,

He renamed her his dear dental Floss.

Copy the limerick in joined writing.
Can you do it in less than 2 minutes?

_____

_____

_____

_____

_____

Evaluation

Are all the letters correctly formed?
Are any letters closed which should be open? (e.g. *h, m, n, s, u, y*)

Are there any words that could be mistaken for another word because of poor letter formation?
Other comments:

Name _____ Date _____

drum   tambourine   clarinet   violin   trumpet   bassoon

French horn   trombone   double bass   oboe   flute   triangle

cello

Copy the instruments into their sections in joined writing. Write in 2 minutes.

strings	woodwind	brass	percussion

Evaluation

Are all the letters correctly formed? Are any letters open that should be closed? (e.g. *a, b, d, e, g, o, p*)

Other comments:

Name   Date

Solve the problem!

*There are 297 millilitres of water in a
jug. If another 785 millilitres are added,
how much water is now in the jug?
If the jug has a capacity of 2 litres,
how much more water could it hold?*

Write the problem in 2 minutes in joined writing.

_____

_____

_____

_____

_____

Evaluation

How well did you space your writing?

Other comments:

Name

Date

Q: How can you tell which
end of a worm is the head?

A: Tickle the middle and see
which end smiles.

Q: What's worse than finding
a maggot in your apple?

A: Finding half a maggot
in your apple.

Can you copy both jokes in joined writing in 2 minutes?

_____

_____

_____

_____

_____

_____

_____

_____

Evaluation

Are spaces between words consistent?

Are words too close together or too far apart?

Other comments:

Name   Date

Make notes about the North Wind and the Sun.

argumentative
wants p.

N.W. pushy -
1st

The North Wind and the Sun were (arguing) about which of them was the most (powerful.) The argument lasted until they spied a traveller crossing the countryside below and they agreed to have a competition to see who could strip him of his clothes.

The (North Wind tried first.) He blew with all his might but the stronger and colder his blasts, the more the traveller gripped his outer clothes. Eventually, the North Wind gave up and challenged the Sun to do better.

The Sun shone out with all her warmth and no sooner did the traveller feel the gentle rays than he took off his overcoat to enjoy the warmth. The Sun continued to shine and the traveller to shed layer after layer of clothes. When he came, hot and perspiring, to a stream he gave a cry of joy, stripped off all his remaining clothes and plunged in for a cooling bathe.

Moral: Gentle persuasion is better than force.

Adapted from Aesop's Fable

Name .... Date ....

Use note-making handwriting to record your ideas.

Scenes		*Dialogue ideas*
	The North Wind and the Sun were arguing about which of them was the most powerful. The argument lasted until they spied a traveller crossing the countryside below and they agreed to have a competition to see who could strip him of his clothes.	
	The North Wind tried first. He blew with all his might but the stronger and colder his blasts, the more the traveller gripped his outer clothes. Eventually, the North Wind gave up and challenged the Sun to do better.	
	The Sun shone out with all her warmth and no sooner did the traveller feel the gentle rays than he took off his overcoat to enjoy the warmth. The Sun continued to shine and the traveller to shed layer after layer of clothes. When he came, hot and perspiring, to a stream he gave a cry of joy, stripped off all his remaining clothes and plunged in for a cooling bathe.	
	Moral: Gentle persuasion is better than force.	

Name .... Date ....

Use information from this policy for your notice. Make notes and underline.

Internet Access and Information Ethics Policy

Why is Internet access important?

The purpose of Internet access by children is to raise educational standards.

◆ Access to the Internet is a necessary curriculum tool for staff and pupils.

Copyright laws

Information which is available on the Internet is not necessarily copyright free and software that the children have at home is not necessarily licensed for school use.

◆ Both pupils and staff are expected to observe copyright regulations in respect of photocopying and electronic copying of material.

◆ Children will be taught to look for copyright information and to respect the intellectual copyright of the authors.

◆ Children should not bring in software or disks from home unless they have been specifically requested to by a teacher, in which case the use of the software will be carefully monitored to ensure that software licences have not been infringed. This action will also protect the school against viruses being imported.

How will Internet use provide effective learning?

Internet access is a necessary part of the statutory curriculum. It is an entitlement for pupils based on responsible use.

◆ Internet access will be planned to enrich and extend learning activities.

◆ Pupils will only have supervised access to the Internet and will always be given clear objectives for Internet use.

◆ Staff will select sites that will support the learning outcomes planned for pupils' age and maturity.

◆ Pupils will be educated in taking responsibility for Internet access.

How will e-mail be managed?

Pupils need to use e-mail in Key Stage 2 as part of the National Curriculum 2000 Orders.

◆ All incoming e-mails can be scrutinised by the teacher.

◆ Children will be told to report immediately if they receive any e-mail which makes them feel uncomfortable.

◆ The forwarding of chain letters will be banned for both pupils and staff, as will the use of chat lines.

Safety

In common with other media such as magazines, books and video, some material available via the Internet is unsuitable for pupils. The school will supervise pupils and take all reasonable precautions to ensure that users access only appropriate material.

Name .... Date ....

Use notes to plan your information notice.

General computer use	Internet access	Using e-mail	Safety

Practice sheet